The

Jenkes

Pierre Birnbaum

Translated by Arthur Goldhammer

The Heights of Power

An Essay on the Power Elite in France

With a New Postscript, 1981

The University of Chicago Press
Chicago and London

Pierre Birnbaum is professor of political sociology at the University of Paris I and the Institut d'Etudes Politiques.

Originally published as *Les sommets de l'Etat,*
©Editions du Seuil, 1977

The University of Chicago Press, Chicago 60637
The University of Chicago Press, Ltd., London

©1982 by The University of Chicago
All rights reserved. Published 1982
Printed in the United States of America
89 88 87 86 85 84 83 82   1 2 3 4 5

Library of Congress Cataloging in Publication Data

Birnbaum, Pierre.
   The heights of power.

   Translation of: Les sommets de l'État.
   Includes bibliographical references and index.
   1. Bureaucracy—France—History. 2. Elite
(Social sciences)—France—History. 3. France—
Constitutional history. I. Title.
JN2681.B5513   354.4401   81-16101
ISBN 0-226-05202-8   AACR2

For Christine

Contents

Translator's Note ix
List of Abbreviations xi

Introduction	1
1 **The State's Claim to Independence** A Model	3
2 **The Power Structure** From Unity to Disunity	14
3 **The Fourth Republic** Increased Separation of Political and Administrative Power	31
4 **The Republic of Functionaries** Towards a New Integration of Politics and the Bureaucracy	45
5 **The Growing Autonomy of Government and Bureaucracy under the Fifth Republic**	65
6 **Government Control over Economic Life**	84
7 **The Giscardian System** The Impossible Fusion of Power and the Decline of State Autonomy	112
Conclusion	138
Postscript, 1981	141
Notes	149
Index	167

Translator's Note

The French text of *The Heights of Power* was composed in 1976, at a time when President Valéry Giscard d'Estaing seemed assured to reelection to another seven-year term as president. As everyone knows, dramatic events intervened. Socialist François Mitterrand was elected president of the Republic in 1981. As a result, the translation may strike the reader in a few places as having been overtaken by events. I have included notes where appropriate to indicate how tensions within Giscardism identified by Professor Birnbaum may have contributed to Giscard's downfall. By and large the text itself has been left intact, except for the occasional addition of a caveat such as "as of this writing." The author's new postscript suggests how the recent changes in France may be related to the arguments developed in the main body of the text.

Quotations from Marx cited in the text were cited in the original from French sources; I have used standard and widely available English translations in rendering these passages. Certain other works cited by the author from French translations were written originally in English; I have cited the original edition. Where French works of which an English translation exists are cited, I have indicated the existence of the translation in the notes; in some cases I followed the existing translation, in other cases I have preferred to provide a translation of my own.

Abbreviations

CDS	Centre de démocrates sociaux (political party)
CEA	Commissariat à l'énergie atomique
CFDT	Confédération française démocratique du travail (union)
CFP	Compagnie française des pétroles
CGE	Compagnie générale d'électricité
CNI	Centre national des indépendants (political party)
CFTC	Confédération française des travailleurs chrétiens (union)
CID UNATI	Comité d'Information et de Défense —Union nationale des travailleurs indépendants (small-business association)
CII	Compagnie Internationale de l'Informatique
CNPF	Conseil national du patronat français (business association)
EGF	Electricité et Gaz de France
ENA	Ecole Nationale d'Administration
ERAP	Entreprise de Recherches et d'Activité petrolière
FORMA	Fonds d'Orientation et de Régularisation des Marchés Agricoles
MRP	Mouvement républicain populaire (political party)
OAS	Organisation de l'Armée secrète

ORTF	Office de la radiodiffusion et télévision françaises
PCF	Parti communiste français (political party)
PME	Confédération générale des petites et moyennes entreprises
RATP	Régie autonome des transports parisiens (runs the Metro)
RFP	Régie pour Favoriser la Productivité
RI	Républicains Indépendants (political party)
RPF	Rassemblement du peuple français (political party)
SFIO	Section française de l'Internationale ouvrière (Socialist party)
SNCF	Société nationale des chemins de fer (French national railway)
SNIAS	Société nationale indépendante pour l'aéro-spatiale
UDR	Union pour la défense de la République (political party)
UIMM	Union des Industries Minière et Mittalingique (trade association)

Introduction

This book is devoted to a study of the governing elite in France, comprising both politicians and bureaucrats. Its ambition is to contribute to a better understanding of the French state. In order to avoid the pitfalls of purely structural approaches, which by piling metaphor upon metaphor contrive to eschew empirical inquiry altogether, and at the same time to skirt the opposite danger of reducing the social system to a collection of individuals acting more or less of their own free will, one must keep in view the idea that the action of the state as an institution depends in large measure on the people who direct it.

There is at present no general work which treats the changing nature of the French political class in the broad sense: the class that includes not only politicians per se, such as members of parliament and cabinet ministers, but also high-level bureaucrats such as cabinet assistants who participate intimately in the implementation of government decisions. This "politico-administrative" elite, then, is markedly heterogeneous. Its membership includes on the one hand professional politicians in the traditional sense and on the other hand high civil servants whose competence is of quite another kind. The relations between these two groups have varied over the course of French history, ranging from open hostility to almost total unity. Accordingly, it would seem that the homogeneity or heterogeneity of the governing elite, which occupies the top posts in government, should be an important factor in determining the cohesion of the state, which can, in effect, be led by a heterogeneous group of individuals representing a wide range of socioeconomic interests. However, this fact is rarely considered by contemporary analysts of the state, and even those who seem aware of it have been quick to gloss over the internal conflict that lies at the root of a profound crisis of government. Some authors, while acknowledging the existence of conflicting interests within the elite, immediately resort to ideological obscurantism and, presto, restore a unity that has not been shown to exist. Others eliminate conflict within the governing elite from the outset, holding that it is merely the expression of a secondary contradiction which does nothing to alter the monolithic nature of the institution.

We shall neither marshall metaphors to show that in fact all the classes find their unity in the state, nor take the contrary tack to show how the different classes are pitted against one another in a battle for control of the government. Rather, it seemed more profitable to analyze the changing faces at the heights of power and to examine whether the ruling elite showed signs of unity or disunity—in both cases, of course, emphasizing the ties between the elite and the various classes or groups within the broader social structure. In short, our ambition is to work from an empirical study of the politico-administrative elite in contemporary France toward posing in fresh terms a problem too often treated in a purely abstract manner: the problem of the functional autonomy of the state.

1   The State's Claim to Independence
A Model

A highly centralized country, France was forged by state action, which exerted a strong homogenizing influence: thanks to such institutions as the bureaucracy, the educational system, the courts, and the army, the state gradually shaped society as a whole in all its aspects. As everyone knows, the power of the state has grown steadily throughout the history of France, and the government has not hesitated to suppress special interests bent on preserving their individual identity. But what exactly is the state in France? A reified concept of the state is widely current. Many writers think of it as an instrument with a will of its own, as a more or less rational creature which organizes civil society on plans of its own devising. From an opposite angle, the critics of monopoly capitalism view the state as a mere tool of the great cartels. As contradictory as these views are, both sides neglect to say what the state is in itself. Neither offers an analysis of the personnel who speak and act in the state's name. In view of the key role that has fallen to the state in French society today, however, we must examine the individuals who direct its actions if we hope to move beyond the opposing theories and make an appreciably new contribution to the study of the conditions influencing the state's autonomy. To a certain extent the autonomy of the state depends on the autonomy of the people who direct it. Even more important, given certain specific historical circumstances, whenever a belief has arisen that the state could rely on the services of a distinct, professionalized group of civil servants, totally identified with their roles because of their "consciousness of serving the public interest,"[1] a claim to more than mere autonomy, indeed to genuine independence, has been advanced in its behalf. In this first chapter we shall examine the state's claim to independence, which has recurred regularly throughout the history of France.

The Example of Bonapartism

To begin with, let us observe that Marx pressed his investigation into the state's claim to independence furthest in his writings on French society, and specifically in his study of Napoleon III. Indeed, Marx noted that "the French bourgeoisie was compelled by its class position to annihilate, on the one hand, the vital conditions of all parliamentary power, and therefore, likewise, of its own, and to render irresistible, on the other hand, the executive power hostile to it."[2] At first, then, the state seemed to escape the control of the economic powers, since the bourgeoisie knew that "in order to save its purse, it must forfeit the crown, and the sword that is to safeguard it must at the same time be hung over its own head as a sword of Damocles."[3] Because the events of 1848 threatened its economic interests, the bourgeoisie agreed to relinquish control of the state in order to be sure of holding on to its economic power. In this way a split occurred between political and economic power, which made it possible for the state to lay claim to independence.

As Marx goes on to say, the bourgeoisie "apotheosized the sword; the sword rules it."[4] After Napoleon III's seizure of power, "the struggle seems to be settled in such a way that all classes, equally impotent and equally mute, fall on their knees before the rifle butt."[5] All classes—including, obviously, the bourgeoisie, which is henceforth willing to content itself with economic power alone. From this date forward, then, all of society became "subordinate" to political power, because Bonaparte, "as the executive authority which has made itself an independent power,"[6] now found himself at "the head" of "the state machine [which] has consolidated its position so thoroughly."[7]

It is possible to interpret Marx's remarks as signifying merely that the state had acquired some measure of autonomy within the capitalist relations of production, thereby enhancing the control exerted by the hegemonic class. But then any attempt to interpret Marx's observations more strictly, as recognizing a real, if temporary, separation between the state and civil society, must be seen as a "play on words."[8] However, the mere autonomy that Marx's interpreters are usually willing to accord to the state is not enough to explain what Marx himself refers to later on as "independence." Even if, as Marx argues, this independence can be explained by the absence of class consciousness among the small-holding peasants, and even if it was only temporary, since in order to govern Napoleon III would need to reach some accommodation with the bourgeoisie, whose support he required, still Marx himself maintains that the independence of the state, or in any case its claim to independence, was based on the functional autonomy of the state apparatus "in a country like France, where the executive power commands an army of officials numbering more than half a million individuals and therefore constantly maintains an immense mass of interests and livelihoods in the most absolute dependence; where the state enmeshes, controls, regulates, superintends and tutors civil society..."[9]

Prominence should be given to the fact that Marx recognizes the independence of the state at the very point in his argument where he is describing the real nature of its functional autonomy: the state, he says, is a machine served by an army of functionaries "pitted against" society, and furthermore in control of a real army, the military. In consequence, as Marx saw it, once the state had truly acquired institutional form, once it had established a distinct and autonomous group of civil servants and professional soldiers to do its bidding, it could move beyond mere autonomy and lay claim to true independence. Curiously enough, Marx, who based his argument on a study of the Second Empire, followed a course previously mapped out by Tocqueville, who emphasized the consequences of the traditional centralization of the French state. Centralization, which began with the absolute monarchy and grew steadily through all the subsequent revolutions, had produced a state "which enmeshes the body of French society like a net."[10] This extreme centralization, which was destined to increase steadily down to the present day, and the creation of an autonomous, self-regulating governmental machinery, fostered a temptation to try and run the whole show from the center, using the resources at the disposal of the state, the source of its "independence."

The governmental bureaucracy, then, is seen as an instrument intended to replace politicians as such and to organize all aspects of life down to its economic foundations: in this light, we can see clearly, for example, the politics behind the great public works undertaken during the Second Empire[11] and the leading role played by the high officials of the bureaucracy, foremost among whom were the prefects, who represented the state in the *départements* and wielded great power to intervene in local affairs. It is true that on several occasions Marx emphasizes that the state does not "soar high above society" and that "under its sway, bourgeois society, freed from political cares, attained a development unexpected even by itself."[12] The bourgeoisie, then, does not control the state and yet ultimately reaps the benefit from this situation, since the government does not interfere with its business affairs. Marx nevertheless went on asserting the state's "domination": uninjured though the interests of the bourgeoisie were by the actions of the state, the state still dominated the bourgeois class while maintaining its own "independence" as a centralized machine in control of two "armies."

Writers discussing these Marxian analyses often emphasize that in the end the bourgeoisie profited from its loss of political power, the "hegemonic" class retaining—though just how it did so is never specified—control over the "governing" class in charge of the machinery of government.[13] And yet, as we shall see later on, it was also possible for the bourgeoisie to retain direct control of the machinery of government and still prosper; to focus exclusively on this one conclusion of Marx's study is to fail to see that Marx understood the full importance of genuine institutionalization of the state apparatus. At a time when bureaucracies, as Weber defined them, were undergoing rapid development, as functional organizations whose members fulfilled more or less rationally the roles assigned to them solely on the basis of their competence, proven by examination, Marx shows that "where the bureaucracy is to become a new principle, where the universal interest of the state begins to become an explicitly singular and thereby a 'real' interest,"[14] the state "constitutes itself as a real power and becomes itself its own material content."[15] Thus Marx emphasizes that the state can use its successful institutionalization in support of its claim to independence as an organization with autonomous interests and personnel. If this key dimension of Marx's analysis of Bonapartism is not kept in view, and the accent is placed instead exclusively on the relative autonomy of the state vis-à-vis the bourgeois owners of the means of production, the importance Marx accords to the emergence of a coherent, functional, and institutionalized state apparatus will be greatly underestimated.

Still, it may be that Marx's analysis overestimates the institutionalization of the state machinery: indeed, the construction of a true bureaucratic machine was far from complete by the end of the Second Empire, and thoroughgoing institutionalization would not be achieved before the second half of the twentieth century. Nevertheless, the process had begun on a wide scale, and Marx intuitively grasped its importance, though he lacked the empirical data available today to underpin his assertions. To understand the trend toward institutionalization, which was to culminate in the Fifth Republic, we must look at both the social background and the professional history of the individuals who came to occupy the top posts in the government. The vast majority of members of the Conseil d'Etat,[16] prefects,[17] directors and secretaries-general of central departments in the bureaucracy,[18] and generals in the military[19] sprang either from the nobility or the high bourgeoisie. The state, then, was controlled by individuals drawn from the most privileged social classes, and initially this made nonsense of its claim to independence. The striking thing, however, is that there was a strong tendency to move toward a professional civil service.[20]

By a wide margin, most of these officials came from families in which the father was already a functionary:[21] from birth, then, their world was the state, and family tradition destined them to serve the state in their turn. We even find in many cases that prefects were sons of prefects and members of the Conseil d'Etat sons of former members. Thus these individuals belonged to important administrative families, whose specific affinities within the bureaucracy would steadily narrow. These families, moreover, had formed many ties among themselves through marriage after marriage, which tended to accentuate the autarchic nature of these institutions.

Finally, their children began their careers in the service of the state: during the Second Empire we find few individuals who first worked in the business world before going into public service. This only increased the functional autonomy of the government and of bureaucratic roles. From this date forward, moreover, such autonomy was deliberately encouraged, by the establishment of higher professional standards for administrative personnel: Napoleon III, for instance, once remarked that "when a country has schools in the arts of law, healing, and war, schools of theology, and so on, is it not shocking that there is no school in the art of government, which is certainly the most difficult art of all, for it takes in all the sciences, exact, political, and moral?"[22] Nor was the attempt during the Second Empire to establish a university course designed to meet the needs of government officials altogether a novelty: in 1848, during the Second Republic, an ephemeral Ecole nationale d'administration (ENA) was founded, in order to provide truly professional instruction to state administrators.[23] Fruitless though these efforts proved, they are nonetheless indicative of a tendency toward institutionalization of the machinery of state. Surely that machinery would continue to serve the interests of the bourgeoisie, and yet it grew into a genuine organization, which on the local level, for example, threatened the power of the notables.[24] The true creation of the ENA, however, would have to await the end of the Second World War, when the Gaullism of the immediate postwar era coincided, as we shall see, with a historical climate not without striking analogies to Bonapartism, so far as the state's claim to independence is concerned.

Gaullism and Its Analysis by the Communist Party

Empirical analysis of the personnel occupying the top posts in government thus turns out to be fruitful, particularly as a way of distinguishing between different historical situations. The first thing that strikes us in comparing Gaullism with the Second Empire is the similarity between the two: in both cases the state declares its independence and attempts to organize society as a whole. Dissimilarities do emerge, however, and these, as was noted earlier, can be explained largely by the greater or lesser degree of institutionalization of the machinery of government.

The State's Claim to Independence

Gaullism has always had the ambition to construct a state independent of the various forces at work within society. In this respect the aim of the Gaullists is similar to that of Napoleon III and, before him, of the absolute monarchs. French history has thus intermittently witnessed the resurgence of a claim to independence on the part of the state. From the outset the theme of independence has held an important place in Gaullist throught about the state. In de Gaulle's speech at Bayeux in June, 1946, the general stated that he wished to appear above the "contingencies of politics" and to serve as a "national arbiter" thanks to his position "above the parties." In article 5 of the 1958 Constitution we again find this idea of the chief of state as arbiter. From the first, the French Communist party rejected the Gaullist state's claim to independence: Henri Claude, for example, argued that the "Gaullist regime, Gaullist politics, and Gaullist ideology are the expression and reflection of monopoly capitalism."[25] For Claude, "direct control of the state by members of the financial oligarchy is a logical consequence of the seizure of economic power by the *grande bourgeoisie:* the concentration of political power is the corollary of the concentration of economic power."[26] By contrast, General de Gaulle tried to tie his own legitimacy to the independence of the state that he led: the ENA was created in 1945 in response to this desire. De Gaulle saw the state as "an institution of decision, an institution of action, and an institution of ambition, solely an expression and a servant of the national interest. If the state is to plan and to make decisions, its authorities must be under the control of a man qualified to judge. If the decisions of the state are to be carried out, it must have at its disposal a capable corps of civil servants, uniformly recruited and trained for the exercise of public office of every kind."[27] Like its predecessors, the Gaullist state thought of its independence as based on an autonomous, functional bureaucracy, which would enable it to carry out its own will. Rejecting the characterization of the regime as one of "state monopoly capitalism," Gaullism aimed to set up a state machinery that would be independent of everyone, and hence of the monopolies as well.

As a way of reviewing the issues briefly before turning to an investigation of the leading figures on the Fifth Republic, we would do well to look at the theoretical conflict that divided the PCF (French Communist party) in 1960 and that was finally settled in early 1961. This debate pitted such important Communists as Casanova, Servin, Pronteau, and Kriegel-Valrimont against the party leadership, and in particular against Maurice Thorez.* One of the most important theoretical debates to occur in the PCF in recent years, it was concerned with the nature of Gaullism and Gaullism's relations with economic power. Though considerations of international politics (the Khrushchev-Thorez opposition, the peace movement, the war in Algeria) and differences over tactics to be followed vis-à-vis the non-Communist left were also involved, essentially two radically divergent interpretations of Gaullism confronted one another.

The party leadership, dominated by Thorez, argued in favor of adherence to point three of the manifesto of the Fifteenth Party Congress of June, 1959, according to which, "with de Gaulle and his government, the state is more completely than ever in the hands of the banks and monopolies." The official view, then, was that the theory of state monopoly capitalism applied admirably to Gaullism, the Gaullist state having no freedom to act independently. The government itself was supposed to be rife with representatives of finance and industry; the hegemonic class and the class in control of the machinery of government were said to be mutually permeable.

Others, however, argued that Gaullism could not be identified in any straightforward way with the interests of international cartels. Starting from this observation, two different lines of argument were developed. One maintained that Gaullism was the representative of a national capitalism hostile to international capitalism. The other contended that the machinery of the Gaullist state had a life of its own. Complementary though these two lines of argument may be, we must consider them one at a time.

To begin with the idea of national capitalism: the proponents of this line of reasoning claimed that the nationalist aspect of Gaullism could be seen quite clearly in the conflict that pitted Antoine Pinay, then minister of finance, against

---

*Then head of the party.—Trans.

the Gaullist line. In this regard, Marcel Servin argued that the French bourgeoisie was divided into "two camps," hostile to one another.[28] Still more explicitly, Michel Hincker described the conflict between the "nationalist" bourgeoisie and the "internationalist" bourgeoisie. The former was represented by Gaullism, which was using its national oil policy, for example, to attempt to build a state capitalism in control of its own productive apparatus. The latter was represented by the international financial oligarchy, afraid of the economic consolidation of a "nationalist" state with which it would have to compete economically, and supported, in the fight against state capitalism, by Antoine Pinay, spokesman for the Confédération générale des petites et moyennes-entreprises (PME), representing small and medium-sized firms, and the conservative right, whose interests were also threatened by the appearance in France of a state capitalism eager to modernize and capable of attacking the anachronistic remnants of small-scale family capitalism. Although this alliance between great international cartels and the PME, with its membership hostile to state capitalism, may appear paradoxical, to some PCF theoreticians it seemed to be a "principal contradiction," which relegated the conflict between the bourgeoisie and the working class to second place.[29]

This position, which won the support of Jean Pronteau and others, led also to the view that the Gaullist state represented not only a specifically French bourgeoisie but also a governmental machinery driven by the "muddle-headed ambitions of technocratic nationalists."[30] Its adherents shared the idea of Gaullism worked out by Serge Mallet, who observed that "the more the economic prerogatives of the state are expanded, the more the 'managers of the machinery of government' will find that their social status pits them against the managers of private industry."[31] On this view, the state follows a policy of its own devising, determined not by a French "nationalist" segment of the bourgeoisie but by the specific strategies of the officials occupying the top posts in the government. Under these conditions the state can lay claim to independence.

Against such arguments Maurice Thorez was quick to raise a vigorous opposition. In his January 15, 1961, speech to the central committee of the PCF at Ivry, he launched a two-pronged attack against both those who maintained that there were two hostile forms of capitalism and those who held that a new and to some extent independent state had come into being. In some measure fusing these two, not quite identical, arguments, he declared that "the error, it must be said, is considerable. How is state capitalism to be severed from the monopolies?" To argue in this vein, he went on, was not far from "making the same mistake that gave rise to the idea of de Gaulle as a reject of one monopolistic faction, or even as standing above the monopolies (why not above the classes?)."[32]

However the twists and turns of this debate may have been affected by international, internal, or even individual strategies,[33] one theoretical problem emerges clearly from it: under what conditions is the state likely to achieve independence? Thorez followed out the logic of his adversaries to the end, charging them with accepting the idea that the machinery of government enabled the state to acquire a certain independence vis-à-vis the cartels.[34] The upshot of this line of argument is the model that we have already encountered in our examination of earlier historical situations:[35] whenever the state lays claim to independence, it does so because it believes it can rely on a governmental machinery controlled by autonomous officials whose interests are linked to the organization in which they hold office. To evaluate this claim, in some respects carrying on the debate that exercised the PCF in 1960–61, an examination of the characteristics of the governing class under the Fifth Republic will prove indispensable. Before proceeding to a lengthy scrutiny of today's new political class, however, we should like first to analyze how the French governing elite has evolved since the nineteenth century, since, as we shall see, the profound transformations of the elite explain the state's claim to independence under the Fifth Republic. Using the model set forth earlier in this chapter, we should like to reexamine, first, certain periods in recent French history during which the total unification of power within the government and bureaucracy on the one hand and the economy on the other made nonsense of any claim to independence on the part of the state; second, other periods during which the total disunity of political, administrative, and economic power greatly hampered the action of the political personnel charged with managing the machinery of government; and, finally, still other periods during which unity was restored in the political and administrative spheres but no in the economic, thus giving rise to fresh claims to independence on the part of the state.

2 The Power Structure
From Unity to Disunity

The Unification of the Three Powers under the July Monarchy

The period of modern French history during which the state could least boast of independence, because it had become an integral part of a homogeneous and powerful ruling class, was, it would seem, the time of the July Monarchy. All power was held by the *grande bourgeoisie:* already dominant economically, it succeeded rapidly in laying hold of political power, as well as in gaining control of the machinery of socialization and information, thanks to which it was able to legitimate its own power.[1] The *censitaire* system of voting qualification (based on standards of property and income) in effect eliminated the middle classes and the "men of talent" from the electoral process: in this period the 250,000 electors were drawn from among the *grande bourgeoisie* and the landowning class.

Despite this favorable combination of circumstances, however, relatively few members of the industrial and commercial bourgeoisie were represented in the Chamber of Deputies. The deputies of 1840 may be classed into four basic professional groups: functionaries (175), landowners without other occupations (137), members of the liberal professions (87), and, finally, representatives of the world of affairs, some 60 in number, only 10 of whom were bankers, 19 manufacturers, and 31 merchants.[2] Thus the number of major commercial and industrial capitalists in the Chamber was small. While it is true that industry (or, rather, finance) was better represented at the ministerial level (Louise-Philippe entrusted the first government of his reign to Jacques Lafitte, a banker, and the second to Casimir Périer, also a banker), still the point to notice is that Thiers, who of course played a key role, was a former journalist with no fortune of his own. The July Monarchy, then, accorded a large role in its ministries to "men of talent": for example, academics such as Guizot, Villemain, and Cousin held positions of the first rank.[3] In control of economic power, the *grande bourgeoisie* did not monopolize all the seats in parliament: it was quite often satisfied to delegate such posts to members of the intellectual elite whose loyalty it had won, or to functionaries it controlled.

Indeed, the percentage of functionaries among the deputies is quite striking, and in this respect the July Monarchy was not very different from the governments of the Restoration,[4] notwithstanding the law of April, 1831, which attempted to reduce the number of functionaries in parliament by laying down certain rules concerning conflict of interest. In the Chamber of 1831, 251 out of 459 deputies were civil servants, 181 of them in the majority; in the Chamber of 1834, there were 276 civil servants out of 459 deputies, 205 of them supporting the government. In 1837, we find 273 functionaries; in 1839, 272; in 1842, 262; and in 1846, 287, with 200 of them on the government side.[5] Thus the number of civil servants in the Chamber of Deputies continued to grow steadily; by themselves they were enough to assure the government an automatic majority. By far the majority of this group accepted jobs closely connected with the executive arm of government. For voting the wrong way some high civil servants were immediately dismissed,[6] while others enjoyed rapid advancement in reward for their steadfast support of the government in the Assembly. Equally worthy of note is the interest members of the Grands Corps showed in participating in parliament during this period: for example, 42 members of the Conseil d'Etat sat in the Chamber of 1846 (35 conservatives, 7 among the moderate opposition), along with 11 members of the Cour des comptes (only one of them in the opposition).[7] Thus the very highest levels of the administration were represented in the Assembly and indeed played a central role there in serving the government.

This invasion of the political sphere by members of the bureaucracy takes on an even greater significance if we look at the reverse phenomenon, also widespread during the July Monarchy: "political life penetrated the administration."[8]

The collusion between political and administrative power was thereby reinforced. As André-Jean Tudesq has observed, the entry requirements and low pay for positions in the Grands Corps meant that these jobs were reserved for notables. Sons of notables, for instance, obtained posts in the Conseil d'Etat thanks to recommendations from politicians; usually, moreover, they were sons of aristocrats or industrialists.[9] The same is true of the Cour des comptes, where outside influence played a crucial role. Similarly, many prefects were drawn from the world of industry.[10]

The high administration, then, had not yet attained functional autonomy: it was either under the thumb of politicians or permeated by the influence of the world of affairs. In exchange, as we have seen, parliament was full of functionaries, who also controlled the *conseils généraux:* two thirds of the members of these bodies were drawn from the ranks of civil servants.[11] Under the July Monarchy, then, we witness a tight integration of the world of affairs with the administration, which in turn controlled parliament. Business was thus represented both in parliament and in the executive, either indirectly through the civil service or directly by individuals who themselves took part in the world of affairs, these being joined in parliament by a very considerable group of landowners. In this period, then, there seems to have been nearly total unity between the business world and the personnel of both the legislature and the administration, which precluded any claim to independence on the part of the state.

The Separation of Powers under the Third Republic: The Professionalization of Politics

By the beginning of the Third Republic this unity in the power structure was coming to an end. As was noted earlier, under the Second Empire the high civil service in particular had been moving toward autonomy, thereby affording the government a certain independence.[12] With the advent of the Third Republic politicians gained control of both the legislative and executive branches and were quick to stake out their own position, thereby promoting complete separation of political, administrative, and economic powers. Particular stress should be laid on the split that developed between politicians and administrators: the upshot of this was an enduring gulf between the political sphere and the high civil service, a gulf which remained until the end of the Fourth Republic.

A new group of politicians climbed their way inch by inch to power owing to the establishment of universal suffrage in 1848, which put an end to the *censitaire* system of electoral qualification that had protected the interests of the major notables. Starting with the provisional government of February 1848, the middle classes, represented by Lamartine, Arago, Ledru-Rollin, Carnot, and others, seized power in an effort to demolish the power of the *grande bourgeoisie*. Despite reverses—such as attempts to place limits on universal suffrage (in 1850, for example, a requirement of three years' residence in the commune was instituted, a measure aimed at preventing workers, who moved often, from voting) or the official candidacies of the Second Empire, which temporarily preserved the power of the notables—and despite resistance in the early days of the Third Republic to the rise of the middle classes and the men of talent, in the end the latter were successful in conquering political power. As Jean Lhomme has observed, the Third Republic ended the rule of the three powers, the *grande bourgeoisie* relinquishing its political power in order to hold on to its economic power and it ability to exercise social control. The establishment of universal suffrage led ineluctably to the separation of powers.[13]

Indeed, it was universal suffrage that gave birth to a new group of politicians who issued from the middle classes and were skilled, as would soon become apparent, at running those newly built political machines, the major parties of the Third Republic. After the "end of the notables" and "the Republic of the dukes" depicted for us by Daniel Halévy, and after the failure of MacMahon, came a new "revolution, just launched, in the form of the spoils system,"[14] the upshot of which would be a complete transformation of the nature of political power.

It is striking to note to what degree the theme, classic in political science, of the steadily increasing professionalization of politics, as set forth by Weber or Mosca or, later, Schumpeter, was already being stated in a very conscious way by political spokesmen of this period. As early as September,

1872, for example, in a speech delivered at Grenoble, Gambetta made the following observation: "Have we not witnessed the emergence all over the country of a new group of politicians, created by universal suffrage.... I announce the advent and the participation in national political life of a new stratum of society."[15] These new politicians represented the "new strata of society" whose principal champion was to be the Radical party. Later, Gambetta added a clarification: "I said new strata, not new classes: 'class' is a bad word, one I never use."[16] Indeed, the nature of universal suffrage made it necessary to downplay social cleavages in formulating party strategy, for those cleavages made it hard to bring together a majority coalition. The new politicians, mainly "men of talent" issuing from the middle classes, therefore adapted their campaign strategy to the requirements of universal suffrage.

Even before Max Weber had analyzed the political calling in his classic "Politics as a Vocation," which appeared in 1919, Robert de Jouvenel could write, in 1914, that "to be a deputy ... is a profession, a profession that has its own customs, its own methods, its own lines of advancement, and almost its own hierarchy."[17] Compared with the practice of the July Monarchy, the change was considerable. Landowners, for instance, had already virtually disappeared from the ranks of officeholders: with France undergoing rapid economic transformation, accompanied by steady growth of the middle classes and the number of capable, educated men, landed wealth was simply steamrollered by universal suffrage. Still more significant, however, is the complete breakup of the civil-servant bloc in parliament, so potent in earlier years. The numbers of high functionaries and, in particular, members of the Grands Corps in parliament diminished steadily during the Third and Fourth Republics, making way for professional politicians brought to the fore by universal suffrage. Unity of the political class was supplanted for a long time to come by disunity and by increasing autonomy for members of parliament, who from this time on were drawn neither from the high levels of the administration nor from the world of industry. Now the state was in the hands of politicians whose interests did not necessarily coincide with those of the high administration or of business circles.

As Radicals saw it, politics was an end in itself: it was autonomous and required specific instruments of its own, such as the Parti républicain radical et radical-socialiste,* founded in 1901, the first major party of national scope in France. Even if the organization of the "machine" still left something to be desired, it was good enough to win elections: the party "militants" were first and foremost politicians,[18] hence professionals of a particular kind. In effect, as André Tardieu observes, the new members of parliament had no "other qualifications but as legislators. They held on to their offices. For if they lost them, they lost everything."[19] This observation should serve as a reminder that power is always based on specific resources, not all of which are necessarily concentrated in the same hands: with regard to the new-style politician, the point is that the kind of man raised to prominence by universal suffrage more often than not possessed neither great wealth nor a high position in the bureaucracy. Accordingly, his seat in parliament was his only access to power, and he owed that seat to his electioneering skills.

As Albert Thibaudet has pointed out, harking back to a distinction drawn even earlier by Maurice Barrès in *Les Déracinés,* the Third Republic witnessed a confrontation between "scholarship students and heirs to fortunes." Therein lies the origin of the separation of powers and thus of a certain pluralism of ruling groups with diverse interests. Foreshadowing the classic works of Schumpeter with astonishing prescience, Thibaudet, in a chapter entitled "The Autonomy of the Political," sets out a series of arguments which were destined to be revived time and again throughout this century and which we find today in works by such men as Seymour Martin Lipset and Robert Dahl. According to Thibaudet, "politics is an autonomous realm, and not the extension or the handmaiden of economics.... In the present economic circumstances, I wonder where better—indeed, where else—to look for the modicum of leisure and public spirit necessary for political life, if not in the party caucuses.... In no case has a major industrialist or merchant in France played the role of a statesman."[20] With great economy of language Thibaudet manages

---

*The official name of the Radical Party.—Trans.

to give a matchless account of the takeover of political power by men originally sprung from the middle classes; at the same time he explains the withdrawal from political life of industrialists and high civil servants, with the latter henceforth quite often evincing hostility to the new politicians within the government.

Max Weber was the first to analyze the causes and consequences of the emergence of this new group of politicians, who would soon attain autonomy. He begins by observing that "politics, just as economic pursuits, may be a man's avocation or his vocation."[21] For Weber, only those who live "by" (and not "for") politics are really engaged in it as a primary profession. Accordingly, as Weber goes on to remark, "nonplutocratic recruitment of interested politicians, of leadership and following, is geared to the self-understood precondition that regular and reliable income will accrue to those who manage politics."[22] This, in effect, was the purpose of the vote taken on November 22, 1906, with no opposition to speak of, which resulted in an increase in pay for members of parliament in France from 9,000 to 15,000 francs, a considerable jump. French deputies could henceforth live "by" politics, as Weber puts it, making politics their profession. It was this vote, in fact, that ended once and for all the plutocratic recruitment of individuals for public office of which the July Monarchy stands as the shining example.

This growing autonomization of the political class, which manifested itself in France with the advent of the Third Republic, also attracted the attention of writers interested in the theory of elites. For Gaetano Mosca, whose beliefs were essentially anticipated by Gambetta and the Radicals, "it cannot be denied that the representative system provides a way for many different social forces to participate in the political system and, therefore, to balance and limit the influence of bureaucracy in particular."[23] Like Thibaudet, he believed that the middle classes had seized political power, because "those classes have always had the upper hand in the controlling cliques of political parties and in electioneering committees...."[24] And like Weber, Mosca was aware that politics was increasingly becoming a distinctive profession in its own right, a profession which in France was practiced by men from the middle classes who had no other source of real power.

Finally, in order to give some idea of the scope of the phenomenon, we should point out how perfectly Schumpeter's observations apply to the politicians of the Third Republic. In his view, "democracy is the rule of the politician.... It is true that, say, businessmen or lawyers may be elected to serve in parliament and even take office occasionally and still remain primarily businessmen and lawyers.... But normally, personal success in politics, more than occasional rise to cabinet office in particular, will imply concentration of the professional kind and relegate a man's other activities to the rank of sidelines or necessary chores.... Politics will unavoidably be a career."[25] Precisely the same point was made earlier by Robert de Jouvenel, Albert Thibaudet, and André Tardieu, when they examined the new type of politician who rose to prominence under the Third Republic.

These new politicians were mainly members of the liberal professions and functionaries of the lower and middle ranks, more often than not teachers at the elementary or the *lycée* levels. Already we can see the fundamental transformation that has taken place in the nature of the political class: under the July Monarchy and the Second Empire, the many functionaries with seats in the Assembly held high-level posts in the civil service and were usually closely allied with the government, which made good tactical use of them. By contrast, under the Third Republic teachers were the foot soldiers in the big battalions of the left-wing parties: this fundamental change deepened the split that had begun to form between the politicians and the high administration. It accentuated the separation of power. Also worthy of note is the fact that under the Third Republic the few high functionaries with seats in parliament almost all belonged to parties of the center or right (see table 2.1).

Besides teachers, politicians in the Third Republic included doctors, lawyers, and journalists (see table 2.2), with the proportion of lawyers steadily declining while that of doctors constantly increased. Doctors, even more than lawyers, could boast of a very solid local base, owing to their client relations: though not having the wealth or prestige of the old notables,

TABLE 2.1 Political Affiliation and Professional Background of Deputies (1898–1940)

Party	Blue-collar workers	White-collar workers	Lower- or middle-level civil servants	Farmers	Elementary-school teachers	Secondary and university teachers	Journalists	Doctors and pharmacists	Lawyers	Senior civil servants	Engineers, architects	Management personnel, private sector	Merchants	Industrialists, entrepreneurs	Corporate officers	Military officers	Clergy	Landowners, renters	Other, and no information	Total deputies	%
Communists	47	18	5	5	6	3	5	2	1	—	—	1	3	—	—	—	—	—	1	97	3.5
Socialistes SFIO[1]	55	33	12	31	36	32	32	29	43	4	8	12	26	9	—	1	—	—	7	370	13.3
Independent socialists[2]	14	5	4	13	2	11	17	14	41	5	7	7	7	9	2	7	—	—	1	169	6.1
Radicals	5	4	6	53	12	54	29	95	176	13	17	4	35	60	5	8	—	2	3	580	20.8
Center-left[3]	8	8	2	67	2	32	22	75	179	23	25	6	26	67	4	14	2	11	4	584	21.0
Moderate[4]	3	5	4	80	5	35	27	64	211	30	33	6	29	92	11	45	7	49	7	747	26.8
Right[5]	2	2	1	12	—	7	4	5	42	11	3	1	2	10	15	28	1	30	1	165	5.9
Unclassifiable[6]	1	2	—	12	—	3	4	7	16	2	3	2	4	5	3	4	—	5	2	74	2.6
Total deputies	135	77	34	273	63	177	140	291	709	88	96	39	132	252	40	107	10	97	26	2786	100
	246			273	1564							463				117		97	26	2786	
	8.8%			9.8	56.1%							16.7%				4.2%		3.5	0.9	100%	

1. Socialistes unifiés, 1898–1919.
2. Including Jeune République, Parti frontiste, Groupe Pelletan.
3. Républicains de gauche, Gauche démocratique, Gauche républicaine.
4. Union républicaine, Union démocratique, Républicains d'Action sociale.
5. Conservatives, Nationalists, etc.
6. Not affiliated, independent.

TABLE 2.2 Social Composition of the Chamber of Deputies

Législature	Year	Blue-collar workers	White-collar workers	Lower- and middle-level civil servants	Farmers	Elementary-school teachers	Secondary and university teachers	Journalists	Doctors and pharmacists	Lawyers	Senior civil servants	Engineers, architects	Management, private sector	Merchants	Industrialists, entrepreneurs	Corporate officers	Military officers	Clergy	Landowners, renters	Other, and no information	Total
Ass. nat.	1871	4	—	1	42	1	—	44	22	237	43	21	1	18	78	6	71	3	104	12	727
1ʳᵉ lég.	1876	5	—	4	45	1	19	26	40	192	52	13	2	20	37	7	25	1	40	4	529
2ᵉ lég.	1877	3	—	4	38	1	15	29	47	202	50	15	1	18	39	5	30	—	48	12	560
3ᵉ lég.	1881	5	—	9	28	2	18	36	51	192	40	15	1	28	40	4	13	3	37	9	534
4ᵉ lég.	1885	12	3	9	37	1	21	37	48	186	45	21	1	19	46	7	30	3	48	10	588
5ᵉ lég.	1889	10	8	2	37	1	25	40	47	174	38	23	1	18	59	10	41	3	49	11	593
6ᵉ lég.	1893	16	8	4	48	3	33	28	66	175	37	22	1	21	48	6	30	3	30	9	588
12ᵉ lég.	1919	24	13	5	53	8	39	45	49	182	22	25	5	19	53	9	38	4	23	8	624
13ᵉ lég.	1924	44	23	5	55	14	43	28	45	162	19	19	6	23	42	5	27	6	12	6	584
14ᵉ lég.	1928	26	19	9	62	15	45	31	61	145	25	25	13	21	63	14	19	4	17	11	625
15ᵉ lég.	1932	27	19	10	47	16	46	41	60	164	24	21	14	22	53	12	11	3	22	5	617
16ᵉ lég.	1936	56	33	16	62	33	44	40	47	121	21	18	12	32	45	6	10	3	24	3	626

1. Including deputies elected in by-elections. Tables 2.1 and 2.2 are extracted from Matei Dogan, "Les filières de la carrière politique en France," *Revue française de sociologie* 8(1967):472–73.

they nevertheless constituted a group of notables of a new kind and were particularly well represented among the Radicals. As parliamentary office assumed an increasingly local character under the *arrondissement* system, which helped to make the deputy the spokesman for the voters in his district alone, rather than for the nation as a whole, the liberal professions, with strong local roots, were able to exert their influence to even greater advantage. Since the arrondissement system greatly limited the possibility of running outside candidates for office, deputies had to look like genuine "locals."

These conditions were less favorable to lawyers than to doctors; as the Third Republic matured, then, lawyers found themselves paying the price, by 1936 dropping to something less than half the number of seats they had once held: they seem to have drifted away from the "real" France.[26] By contrast, teachers and doctors doubled their representation, with grade-school teachers and petty bureaucrats increasing theirs by a factor of thirty. Lawyers, doctors, and *lycée* teachers, especially representative of the new politics, belonged mainly to the Radical party, and before long would come to be seen as local political notables. The grade-school teachers and petty bureaucrats, on the other hand, swelled the ranks of the left-wing parties such as the Socialists and Communists, and they were more closely tied to these important national organizations than the Radical deputies were to theirs, the Radicals typifying the profoundly "local" character of parliamentary office.

The new notables, whether of Radical stripe or center-right, also benefited from the increasingly stable composition of the Assembly: in 1936, for example, the average member of parliament counted twelve consecutive years in office.[27] Thus the politicians produced by universal suffrage may be characterized as follows: in the main, they were members of the liberal professions or civil servants of modest rank, completely devoted to their party roles and enjoying very stable tenures of office, owing to repeated reelection from the same arrondissement, almost always the district in which they were born, where they started out by holding local elective posts, even before being elected deputies. More than two-thirds of the deputies elected between 1900 and 1940 held seats on town or regional councils.²⁸ The Third Republic thus fostered a specific career path, which accentuated the local character of the parliamentary office: representatives at the national level were first elected to hold seats on their *conseils municipaux* or *départementaux*.

It was from among the ranks of such politicians that ministers were chosen for government, a government that was truly, as André Siegfried would have it, the "mirror"²⁹ of parliament. Hence ministers, too, followed this same career path, which took them by stages from local elective office to positions in the executive branch. In this way the new political class preserved its homogeneity: this would not always be the case in the future. While great notables in the traditional sense are still found at the beginning of the Third Republic,³⁰ they were soon to disappear from parliament as well as government. Unlike regimes in which power exhibits a marked degree of unity, the division of power instituted by this political system would in effect prevent industry and the high administration from controlling political power. Like deputies, ministers were drawn mainly from the liberal and teaching professions (table 2.3). By the same token, practically all the presidents of the Republic were either lawyers or former teachers. Gambetta, Camille Pelletan, and Jules Grévy were lawyers; Clemenceau and Combes were doctors, Herriot and Daladier *agrégés* in literature and history.³¹

Despite the marked separation of powers under this regime, certain differences do emerge between the individuals in parliament and those who rose from its ranks to become ministers. High-level functionaries, for example, are better represented in the executive than in parliament, and lawyers, too, held their own there, while on the other hand the proportion of doctors in the executive was less than half what it was in parliament, and that of grade-school teachers considerably smaller (see tables 2.3 and 2.4).³² In addition, fewer ministers than members of parliament had studied medicine, and none, or almost none, had left school after completing the primary grades, as 20 percent of the deputies had done; furthermore, 16 percent of the ministers had attended the Ecole Polytechnique, Saint-Cyr (the military academy), or the Ecole Navale, whereas only 4 percent of the members of parliament had

TABLE 2.3 Educational and Occupational Background of Ministers under the Third Republic (1870-1940)

	Blue-collar workers	White-collar workers	Lower- and middle-level civil servants	Farmers	Elementary-school teachers	Secondary and university teachers	Journalists	Doctors and pharmacists	Lawyers	Senior civil servants	Engineers, architects	Management personnel, private sector	Merchants	Industrialists, entrepreneurs	Corporate officers	Military officers	Landowners, renters	Others	Total	%
Law	—	—	—	—	—	11	12	—	216	14	—	—	1	6	2	2	1	1	266	42.2
Law, Letters, or Political Science	—	—	—	—	—	16	6	—	24	15	—	—	—	—	—	2	1	—	64	10.2
Letters	—	—	1	—	—	28	10	—	—	3	—	1	—	—	—	—	1	—	44	6.9
Medicine	—	—	—	—	—	2	1	32	—	—	—	—	—	1	—	—	—	—	36	5.6
Science	—	—	—	—	—	7	—	—	—	—	—	—	—	2	—	—	—	—	9	1.4
Ecole Polytechnique, St-Cyr, Navale	—	—	—	—	—	3	—	—	—	5	16	—	—	2	3	69	—	—	98	15.5
Centrale, Mines, Arts et Metiers	—	—	—	—	—	2	2	—	—	1	11	1	—	—	—	—	—	—	14	2.3
d'inst.	—	—	—	—	3	—	—	—	—	—	—	—	—	—	—	—	—	—	5	0.8
Secondary level	—	3	2	4	—	—	11	—	1	10	—	—	8	15	6	—	2	4	64	10.2
Technical schools	—	—	1	—	—	1	1	—	—	2	1	—	—	1	—	—	—	2	11	1.8
Primary schools	4	2	—	3	—	—	4	—	—	—	—	—	2	2	1	—	—	—	17	2.7
No information	—	—	—	—	—	—	—	—	—	—	—	—	—	—	—	—	—	—	3	0.5
Total ministers	4	5	4	8	3	70	47	32	241	50	28	2	11	30	12	73	4	7	631	100

Tables 2.3 and 2.4 are extracted from Matei Dogan, "Les filières de la carrière politique en France," pp. 478-79.

TABLE 2.4 Educational and Professional Background of Deputies (1898–1940)

	Blue-collar workers	White-collar workers	Lower- and middle-level civil servants	Farmers	Elementary teachers	Secondary and college teachers	Journalists	Doctors and pharmacists	Lawyers	Senior civil servants	Engineers, architects	Top managers, private sector	Merchants	Industrialists	Corporate officers	Military officers	Clergy	Landowners, renters	Other, and no information	Total	%
Law	—	—	3	22	2	25	17	—	648	31	1	4	1	23	6	5	—	12	2	802	28.5
Law and Letters	—	—	—	2	—	27	9	—	56	14	—	1	1	5	2	1	1	3	—	122	4.4
Letters	—	—	1	—	2	78	9	—	1	5	—	1	1	—	1	—	9	2	—	108	3.9
Medicine, pharmacy	—	—	—	1	—	5	2	291	1	—	3	1	—	3	—	—	—	—	—	304	10.9
Science	—	—	—	—	—	19	—	—	—	—	3	—	—	2	—	—	—	—	—	24	0.9
Polytechnique, St.-Cyr, Navale	—	—	—	—	—	2	3	—	—	5	12	1	—	6	1	84	—	1	—	115	4.9
Centrale, Mines, Arts et Metiers	—	—	—	—	—	—	—	—	—	1	69	—	1	10	1	—	—	—	—	92	3.3
Ecoles normales d'instituteurs	—	—	—	1	56	5	2	—	1	1	—	—	1	6	—	—	—	2	—	70	2.7
Secondary level	1	5	10	1	1	10	—	—	2	25	—	8	1	10	20	15	—	67	6	395	14.2
Technical schools	2	4	1	44	2	2	55	—	—	2	11	11	23	2	4	1	—	2	—	97	3.5
Primary schools	132	68	19	10	—	4	27	—	1	5	—	6	12	111	3	1	—	1	1	527	18.7
No information	—	—	—	169	—	—	14	—	—	—	—	8	69	22	3	—	—	7	17	130	4.7
Total deputies	**135**	**77**	**34**	**273**	**63**	**177**	**140**	**291**	**709**	**88**	**96**	**39**	**132**	**252**	**40**	**107**	**10**	**97**	**26**	**2786**	**100**

done so. In the same vein, even though the separation of powers in this system was marked, still there was a comparatively large number of high-level functionaries in the government, whereas doctors and grade-school teachers are far less well-represented in the executive: the government did not precisely "reflect" the composition of parliament, and these slight differences would increase steadily until they became distinguishing characteristics of a newly unified regime under the Fifth Republic, for example. In effect, high-level functionaries took over more and more ministerial posts, though their number in parliament remained quite small.

It is true that in this republic of lawyers and teachers certain representatives of major industrial and banking interests such as Henri Germain and François de Wendel continued to sit in parliament alongside representatives of the "new strata."[33] Accordingly, in the view of Daniel Halévy, Gambetta's Republic "kept [the proletariat] out"; it looked much more like the "Republic of Schneider, Dubochet, and Boucicaut."[34] It has been said that the Radicals "allowed the major economic effort launched during the Second Empire of bringing France into the world of capitalism to be rubber-stamped by people who, for a variety of reasons, had been hostile or indifferent to it in the time of Napoleon III."[35] It still remains to be seen why and above all how these Radicals could have become "allies" of big business "even when [they] had a tradition of fighting it politically."[36] Here, in one sentence, we find acknowledgment both of the autonomy of the political and at the same time of the subservience of politicians, of their limited freedom of action.

Still, it would seem that, hitherto at any rate, no historian has specified the nature and form of this supposed dependence, which has been more proclaimed than demonstrated. Nicos Poulantzas turned his attention to a similar set of problems: using such concepts as "hegemonic class" and "governing class," he acknowledged that the Radicals who held political power were distinct from the hegemonic class, but moved from there to the assertion that despite their distinctiveness the Radicals were only "messenger boys" for the hegemonic class, an assertion for which no proof of any kind is offered,[37] and, furthermore, that financial capitalists, as one segment of the hegemonic class, succeeded "through a complex process" in establishing their "control" over parliament.[38]

It would seem that the full measure of the functional separation to which Jean Lhomme in particular has drawn attention has not been appreciated. In a system in which resources are distributed among many hands, and in which universal suffrage has fostered the growth of organized politics practiced by professional politicians essentially without financial resources of their own and having their own political interests to defend, political power is in large part self-determing. At a later date, the Fourth Republic will exemplify the unpredictability of the political class when it has control of the machinery of government; this class, distinguished from the business class in such fundamental respects as social origins and cultural traditions, exerted little control over business and industry, but by the same token was quite impervious to the wishes of that sector of society.

Under the Third Republic politicians also had to contend with personnel in the high administration, from which they had managed to separate themselves without thereby achieving domination over the bureaucracy. To this state of affairs Gambetta gave voice when he said that "the administration must be completely republican, and it will be, because I do not think the country is of a mind to put up for long with the spectacle of a government desired and acclaimed by all of France and thwarted only by its functionaries."[39] This statement of Gambetta's, which would be unthinkable under the Fifth Republic, clearly illustrates the difficulties the "new strata" faced in regard to the high administration, which continued to draw its officials from among the great notables. Even after the Conseil d'Etat had been to some degree purged, the vast majority of *auditeurs* and half the *maîtres des requêtes* continued to be drawn from the high bourgeoisie and the aristocracy.[40] The Grand Corps, such as the Conseil d'Etat, the Inspection des Finances, and the Cour des comptes, assured the *grande bourgeoisie* of continued power within the machinery of government, enabling it to mount an opposition to the new middle-class politicians.

Founded by Emile Boutmy just after France's defeat in 1870, the Ecole libre des sciences politiques accepted the children of the *grande bourgeoisie* and took as its mission the training of new elites, from whose ranks the members of the Grands Corps would be recruited.[41] The composition of the Grands Corps seldom changes: thus, at the end of 1877, more than two-thirds of the prefects had been named by the *Ordre moral,* the vast majority of them being former subprefects of the Second Empire, with more than half claiming aristocratic titles. Down to the end of the Third Republic, there were practically no attempts to purge the prefectural corps, and even the Popular Front made no wholesale changes.[42] The same is true of the high posts in the military: at the beginning of the Third Republic, nine-tenths of the generals in command of divisions and three-quarters of the senior officers were royalists or Bonapartists.[43] At the turn of the century, the old traditional families were strongly represented in high army circles, which were accordingly in close contact with conservative milieux.[44]

Robert de Jouvenel has given us a fine picture of the antagonism between ministers and senior civil servants that prevailed in the Third Republic.[45] Indeed, it could not have been otherwise:[46] the separation of powers had given rise to a marked differentiation, previously unknown but destined to continue long thereafter, between politicians and senior bureaucrats, who together controlled all the key posts in the machinery of state. Their social origins, their cultural background, and their specific career patterns all helped to distinguish one from the other, the more so in that few people shifted from one group to the other. While businessmen, as we shall see later on, have always been relatively underrepresented in French governments, this split between politicians (members of parliament and ministers) and senior civil servants was not destined to last forever.

3   The Fourth Republic
Increased Separation of Political and Administrative Power

Members of Parliament and Their Professional Development

The split between politicians and senior civil servants was also characteristic of the Fourth Republic, which in this respect is scarcely distinguishable from the Third. Once again, the "Republic of deputies" emerged triumphant, the deputies being recruited from among the same social groups as under the Third Republic (see table 3.1). In the Fourth Republic deputies were mainly doctors, lawyers, and teachers (in an even greater proportion than under the Third Republic). However, the entry into parliament of a rather considerable proportion of workers and low-level civil servants should be noted, most of them belonging to the major left-wing parties, such as the PC (Communists) and SFIO (Socialists). The Resistance led to some changes in the country's political complexion after the Second World War, and these changes were reflected in a strengthening of the parties of the left in parliament: highly organized, these parties were mainly composed of militant workers, office employees, and teachers. On the other hand, prominence should be given to a small proportion of senior civil servants among the deputies, still smaller, in fact, than under the Third Republic: the separation of political and administrative power had widened even further. Moreover, the few senior functionaries who did hold seats in the Assembly belonged to parties of the center or right, whose role was less important than it had been under the Third Republic. The increasing thrust of the middle classes and workers into the political ranks both nationally and locally contrasts sharply with the withdrawal of senior civil servants from politics.[1]

TABLE 3.1 Socioprofessional Background of Deputies in the Fourth Republic (1945–58)

	Unclassifiable	PC	SFIO	MRP	Radicals	Moderate independents	RPF	Poujadists	Extreme right	Total
Blue-collar workers	—	99	11	21	—	1	1	—		133
White-collar workers	1	37	16	19	2	—	—	—		71
Petty bureaucrats	—	7	15	5	3	1	—	—		31
Farmers	5	29	10	29	11	40	12	—		136
Elementary teachers	1	29	32	1	2	—	—	1		66
Secondary and college teachers	4	12	35	21	13	7	7	—		99
Journalists	2	5	19	17	12	6	2	1		64
Doctors, pharmacists	—	3	13	15	13	8	10	3		65
Lawyers	8	2	28	25	28	38	11	2		142
Senior civil servants	4	3	4	9	8	6	7	1		42
Engineers	9	4	5	11	8	9	8	—		54
Middle management	3	3	9	14	4	7	2	1		43
Merchants	—	1	2	15	5	6	6	29		64
Industrialists	3	—	2	9	14	16	18	6		68
Military officers, clergy	1	1	—	3	1	6	6	—		18
Miscellaneous	—	11	—	2	—	1	1	—		16
Total—Metropolitan France	41	246	201	216	124	152	91	44		1112
Percentage: distribution	3	22	18	20	11	14	8	4		100

From Matei Dogan, "Political Ascent in a Class Society: French Deputies 1870–1958," in Dwaine Marvick, ed. *Political Decision-Makers* (New York: The Free Press, 1961), p. 67.

Between 1871 and 1958 the new type of politician brought into the limelight by universal suffrage increased his hold on political power. Under the Third and Fourth Republics deputies followed identical patterns in their careers, moving from local elective offices to the National Assembly: thus two-fifths of the deputies of the Fourth Republic had first been members of local councils.[2] The deputies of the Fourth Republic, like those of the Third, enjoyed considerable stability in office: 43 percent of them were reelected five times.[3] Finally, it is worth pointing out the relative decline of owners of means of production, industrialists in particular, in parliament; the rise of the left-wing parties, which deepened the split between administrative and political power, also tended to keep out representatives of industry, which saw its direct control of the machinery of government decline steadily.

As under the Third Republic, the government continued to mirror the parliament more or less faithfully: in this parliamentary regime, the members of the government all came from the Assembly, of which they were in many cases merely the spokesmen. This is why lawyers, journalists, doctors, and teachers continue to be the socioprofessional groups best represented in government (table 4.2). Just as under the Third Republic, however, the proportion of senior civil servants, quite small in the Assembly, is markedly higher in the government. The upshot of this unequal distribution of ministerial powers, under the Fourth Republic as previously under the Third, was to distort the reflection of parliament in the government, slightly lessening the separation between the politicians and the senior civil servants. Then, too, workers, who were represented quite well in the Assembly, had almost no representation in the government; many of them belonged to the PC, moreover, which shared but rarely in the exercise of power.

Ministers were still drawn from parliament, however, as they had been under the Third Republic; thus, by the end of the second legislative session in 1955, 151 of the 541 deputies from metropolitan France, or some 29 percent, had been associated with the executive branch for terms of varying lengths.[4] Despite some minor differences, then, the composition of parliament and government was largely homogeneous: every, or nearly every, member of parliament was seen as ministerial material. Lacking the great wealth and prestige of the traditional notables, these new notables had local roots, and some of them followed the now standard course which led them from their local beginnings to parliament and thence to the government: René Coty, for example, was first a lawyer in Le Havre before winning election, in turn, to seats in his *conseil d'arrondissement,* the *conseil municipal* of Le Havre, the Chamber of Deputies, and the Senate, subsequently becoming a minister and finally present of the Republic.

The consequences of this consolidation of power by the politicians, whose resources were limited to their electioneering skill—a process that began with the Third Republic—do not seem to have been sufficiently appreciated. In order to evaluate the prestige and influence of holding office in parliament or the government, we have compared the occupation and social position of ministers and deputies prior to their election or nomination with the occupation and social position to which they returned after being voted out of office or dismissed from the government. In this way we were able to gauge the effects of holding office on a man's influence in the community, particularly in walks of life other than politics. Our study, unlike anything done before it, focused on deputies turned out of office at the expiration of the 1951–56 legislature, a group typical of parliament in the Fourth Republic.[5] We also looked at all the ministers of the Fourth Republic, some 129 persons in all.[6] As we shall now try to make clear, the results fully confirm both that the political class is a homogeneous group and that it is estranged from big business (firms of national as opposed to local scope).

Looking first of all at the sample of 87 deputies not reelected at the expiration of their term, it is striking that only 11.4 percent of them were named to positions on the boards of directors of firms of national scope after their defeat. Even though the parliament of the Fourth Republic continued to play an essential constitutional role, it seems to have lost any semblance of intimate contact with the world of business, which would have manifested itself by large numbers of former deputies switching to important posts in business. The powers-that-be in the business world, however, evidently did not regard these former deputies as people whose services they required, whereas they were quite willing to open doors to any senior civil servant wishing to leave government, who would bring with him talents worthy of handsome recompense in the business world. Furthermore, access to a seat on the board of a national firm, it turns out, does not correlate with the holding of office in parliament.

In the first place, the number of deputies sitting on such boards depends on what end of the political spectrum is being looked at: the observed distribution depends very strongly on party label. In fact, we find that, of the ten board seats, six were held by members of the RPF, two by independents, one by a Radical, one by a member of the MRP, and none by Socialists. Under the Fourth Republic, Radicals and Socialists had an incomparably greater share in the decisions of the Assembly than did deputies of the RPF. What this first distribution shows, then, is that the link between political and economic power is structured at the party level far more than at the institutional level, that is, the level of parliament itself.

Furthermore, those deputies who were originally industrialists or senior civil servants, few though they were in the Assembly, obtained proportionally the largest number of board positions with firms of national scope. This explains why the typical deputy of the Fourth Republic naturally had no place in the major centers of economic decision-making.

On the other hand, a rather large number of deputies not returned to office took up posts in local firms after leaving the Assembly. Within his district, then, the deputy acquires prestige, influence, and even power from his office. After his defeat he can reap the benefits his old position afforded by conferring on him the status of a notable and the role of an intermediary between local interests and the central government. Ties to management in these cases seem to correlate rather strongly with the individual's having held parliamentary office: we find, for instance, that the longer an individual has held office, the more likely he is to obtain a management position. The stronger a deputy's local roots, the more likely he is to obtain a seat on the board of a local firm: being a deputy definitely carries weight locally. Furthermore, the likelihood of obtaining such a post is now distributed among the various parties in a far more equitable way: in contrast to the situation with national firms, here we find deputies of virtually every political stripe. Only the RPF is not represented, because its deputies had been in politics only a relatively short time: this is also a sign of the unique position of this party, which had close ties with big businesses of national scope.

Finally, the socioprofessional background of deputies taking jobs with local firms differs markedly from that of deputies obtaining seats on the boards of national firms. The latter came primarily from the world of industry and from the senior levels of the bureaucracy: thus apart from their seat in parliament they were already influential on the national level. By contrast, the former came from many different walks of life: we find ten farmers, eleven professionals, two company presidents. Proportionally, farmers more than any other group were offered management posts with local agencies or firms (58.8 percent of the farmers in our sample). This overrepresentation of farmers brings out the deeply local character of the parliamentary office, which has little hold over economic power on the national level but is rather firmly established locally.

Furthermore, it should be noted that former deputies are offered management jobs in precisely those local firms or agencies which have the greatest need to be heard by the national government and the *départemental* bureaucracy. These include mainly public or semipublic agencies whose activities are limited to a town, a canton, or, less often, a *département,* such as agencies in charge of providing low-cost housing, electricity cooperatives, water and highway authorities, and local development committees. In the private sector we find primarily local agricultural and wine cooperatives. Former deputies often hold posts in several such organizations, which are not to be confused with industrial or commercial enterprises of even so much as regional scope. At best the former deputy takes on the role of intermediary, continuing his position as a local notable; this role cannot, however, mask the ever more glaring lack of any contact between elected officials on the national scene and the world of business.

To evaluate the weight carried by parliamentary office under the Fourth Republic we may look, finally, at the professional development of deputies turned out of office. Once again, the absence of any very structured ties between deputies and the business world no doubt explains the low job mobility of former deputies. In other words, we have looked at the advancement, or lack of it, of former deputies in their new careers, and classified them by six characteristics: regression, stagnation, retirement, improvement of professional status, change of profession, career in politics.[7] Around two-thirds of the former deputies did not benefit at all from having held office: though we find no cases of regression, stagnation is by far the dominant phenomenon. Improvement of professional status is not very common (6 percent); in the same vein there are some changes of profession implying a certain rise in status (5 percent). These relatively few cases of improvement are independent of party affiliation and seem to be connected more with the length of term in office. Lack of mobility is found particularly among deputies of modest social status, especially low-level civil servants; this confirms the lack of importance of a seat in parliament in itself.

It should be noted, however, that 20 percent of the former deputies continued in their political careers: this rather high percentage tended to make politicians as a group even more homogeneous, since they were cut off from other sources of power but managed nevertheless to preserve their own professional identity. Political careers were not chosen by farmers, professionals, or company presidents, but mainly by low-level bureaucrats and teachers, almost all of whom belonged to the highly structured parties on the left, such as the SFIO. Party militancy, then, particularly on the left, seems to have contributed to advancement in politics. It was mainly elementary teachers and low-level civil servants who moved from holding office as left-wing deputies to positions as officials of their parties, thus launching political "careers."

To conclude our analysis of the professional development of former members of parliament, we must mention the accelerated career advancement enjoyed by senior civil servants at this time. Their small numbers in the Assembly notwithstanding, 50 percent of these senior functionaries benefited professionally from having held office. Because this figure is so large, we decided to study the advancement of senior civil servants as a phenomenon in its own right. Wherever we looked, we found evidence of a career boost: improvement of professional status (25 percent), rise to a new profession of higher status (12.5 percent), political career (3.8 percent). For a civil servant a stint in parliament meant a leg up in the hierarchy of power. Compare this observation with what we noticed earlier: rare though senior functionaries were in parliament, a far higher proportion of such officials was to be found in the government. Under the Fourth Republic, then, senior civil servants did well by entering the political fray.[8]

Stress has been laid in the course of our analysis on the relatively unimportant part played by parliament in dealing with the major economic decisions facing the nation, as well as in determining the course of business activity; we have also seen how the deputy functioned as an intermediary between the local and the national sphere, and thereby acquired the status of a notable in his own district; and, finally, we have seen how parliament served to "select" certain left-wing militants and senior civil servants for membership in the political elite. By and large, politicians of the new stripe had to content themselves with a more or less brief stint in power: the separation of political, administrative, and economic powers made it difficult if not impossible to extend the range of their influence. We can see, then, how under the Fourth Republic politicians were cut off from other sources of power, over which, when all is said and done, they exerted little control: their freedom of action was diminished in consequence.

The Professional Development of Ministers

Since the government was supposed to "mirror" parliament, we thought it would be interesting to look at former ministers and analyze their careers in the same way as those of deputies. What we found was, first of all, that, like former deputies, former ministers of the Fourth Republic seldom obtained seats on the boards of directors of firms of national scope, whether public or private. Out of a sample of 129 former ministers, 78 percent had no connections with such firms, 3.9 percent kept seats they had obtained before entering parliament, and only 13.5 percent obtained seats after leaving the government.[9] In spite of having held high office, then, former ministers still found themselves cut off from the world of business. Like most deputies, they issued from the middle classes and the liberal professions, which had few close connections with large-scale industry. Nor did their education at school and university prepare them for posts in big business.

The few ministers who did obtain seats on the boards of major firms after leaving office were recruited, like former deputies who obtained such seats, on the basis of party affiliation: 12.5 percent from the SFIO, 11 percent from the Radicals, 16.5 percent from the MRP, 16 percent from the independents, and 32 percent from the RPF. Once again, just as in the case of deputies, the left was discriminated against, and the right, especially the RPF, favored. As we shall see later on, this tendency only increased under the Fifth Republic, with the UDR taking the place of the RPF in profiting from this kind of mobility.

When we look at the professional background of former ministers who ended up on the boards of national firms, we find that the greatest benefits went mainly to senior civil servants and company presidents, small though their numbers were. Now, both these groups were particularly well represented in the ranks of the RPF. On the other hand, teachers, the typical politicians of the Fourth Republic, had few ties to the business world. Many, of course, were members of the leading left-wing parties and old-line militants who reached the top ranks of government, whereupon they deliberately refused to have anything to do with the world of industry. This remark does not apply, however, to the members of the liberal professions, who were well represented in all the parties and yet almost never managed to establish close relations with big business after becoming ministers. Once more this shows that deputies and ministers alike were cut off from other sources of power. On the other hand, it also underscores the very special place of senior civil servants, even as early as the Fourth Republic, top bureaucrats being almost the only individuals who managed to utilize their stint in office as a springboard to a career in the private sector.[10]

What these analyses of the professional development of politicians show, then, is that under the Fourth Republic power was divided, as we have stressed throughout this chapter. The new prominence of politicians of rather modest socio-professional background, often with no resources other than their expertise as professional politicians, opened a radical breach between different kinds of power: for the time being politicians were kept out of power in both business and the administration.

The Technocratic Temptation and the Senior Civil Service

To the question "Who governs France?" André Siegfried, writing in the heyday of the Fourth Republic, answered, "an aristocracy of technical competence,"[11] referring to the senior civil service. In his view, the politicians had not won the war that Gambetta had long ago promised to wage, it will be recalled, against the bureaucracy; faced with the power of the new social strata, the senior bureaucrats managed to hang on to their own preeminence by claiming an expertise quite different from that of the politicians, namely, the mastery of scientific knowledge of a particular kind, which they claimed could be used for managing the social system as a whole.

Just as under the Third Republic, the senior bureaucrats were not very receptive to politicians issuing from the new strata who rose to political power as a result of universal suffrage. Among *inspecteurs des Finances* in 1952, 11 percent came from the aristocracy or *grande bourgeoisie,* 20 percent were sons of industrialists or bankers, 29 percent were sons of men who were themselves senior functionaries. These proportions would hold steady throughout the Fourth Republic, with the last category even increasing its share significantly.[12] Although the *petite bourgeoisie* did manage gradually to gain access to the senior civil service after the creation of the ENA, this did not reduce the dominant part played by individuals who were recruited largely from the business world and the social elite, even though there was also considerable recruitment from within the ranks of the civil service itself. With the apparent exception of the prefectural corps, whose recruits were more heterogeneous,[13] the Grand Corps all resembled the Inspection des Finances in this respect.[14]

These senior bureaucrats, utterly different from the professional politicians, cut off in every way from the deputies—office workers, teachers, doctors, and lawyers—and ministers of similar background, were by this time all trained by a single school, the ENA, which imparted a uniform view of the world, superb competence, and an acute awareness of their own effectiveness, which they looked upon as something politically neutral; subscribing unreservedly to the idea that it is possible to serve "the public interest," which it was their job to define and administer, these officials lived in a world apart and were distrustful of the political process, which they often regarded as reflecting the power of special interests.

Protected by the civil service law of 1945, selected on the basis of high-level examinations that accentuated cultural differences between them and the politicians even further, and assured of secure careers and promotion according to impersonal rules, senior functionaries had by this time become part of a truly institutionalized civil service. Under the Fourth Republic the steady institutionalization of the civil service reached its climax, freeing the bureaucracy once and for all from the threat of political interference. We have come a long way from the time when, as under the July Monarchy, a senior official who happened to be a deputy could jeopardize his career by voting against the government. Covered by a protective law and enjoying tremendous job security and enormous prestige owing both to their elite backgrounds and their technical competence, the senior civil servants form a distinct professional group, whose views on almost every point are at odds with the views of that other important group of professionals, the politicians. Thus two different concepts of the profession of statecraft are in constant danger of clashing with one another.

The possibility of a clash became increasingly likely during the Fourth Republic, when ministerial staffs were filled mainly with senior civil servants. In contrast to the Third Republic—when staffs were still made up largely of personal friends of the minister, who often lacked any special qualifications for their jobs[15]—staffs during the Fourth Republic consisted chiefly of senior functionaries:[16] inspecteurs des Finances, for example, played a large part,[17] along with members of the Conseil d'Etat,[18] the Cour des comptes,[19] and the prefectural corps.[20] Although many writers claim that bureaucrats in the ministries play a purely technical role, still it seems clear that the behavior of politicians is governed by a logic quite different from that which governs the behavior of the civil servant. Both groups are professionalized, but along quite different lines, and clashes are inevitable when the question pertains, say, to evaluating a decision in relation to a campaign strategy, a certain concept of public service, or an advanced view as to the meaning of economic development.

During the Fourth Republic the staffs of the *présidents du Conseil* played an important part in determining the future careers of senior civil servants, especially members of the Grands Corps. If we look at the socioprofessional background and career history of the 1975 functionaries who served on these staffs under the Fourth Republic (or some 82 percent of the membership of the cabinets in question),[21] we find that the *présidents du Conseil* were surrounded almost entirely by functionaries, who were often sons of functionaries, and who in 38 percent of the cases were themselves members of the Grands Corps, i.e., the Inspection des Finances, the Conseil d'Etat, the Cour des comptes, the prefectural corps, and the diplomatic corps. The cabinets of the *présidents du Conseil* of the Fourth Republic—the *présidents* themselves being professional politicians—thus included even more members of the Grands Corps than all the ministerial staffs;[22] both remained closed to the private sector and, in particular, to industry.

It is interesting to look at the professional development of the members of these staffs, because their staff role played an undeniable part in their later careers (see table 3.2). For example, we find that almost all the members of the three Grands Corps (Conseil d'Etat, Inspection des Finances, Cour des comptes) who served on these staffs subsequently came to hold positions in other areas for one period of time or another, and in particular took up posts in industry, both public and private (especially in banking and manufacturing). The same is true to a lesser degree for members of the prefectural corps and the corps of engineers. It should be noted, moreover, that some corps members came to hold political office, thus beginning, even as early as the Fourth Republic, to threaten the almost total domination of the traditional politicians.

The senior civil service, which held its own against both industry and politics, thus used the ministerial staffs as springboards to other areas of control. However, the danger was that both the power of the bureaucrats and their close contacts with other sectors would bring them into conflict with

TABLE 3.2 Career Mobility of Civil Servants on Staffs of Présidents du Conseil under the Fourth Republic

	a	b	c	d	e	f	g
Inspection des Finances	22	7	3	7	4	1	22
Cour des comptes	6	3	1	0	2	0	6
Conseil d'Etat	15	0	0	5	7	1	13
Prefectoral corps	29	0	0	9	3	1	13
Diplomatic corps	9	0	0	1	2	0	3
Corps of engineers	9	1	1	4	2	0	8
Army	11	1	0	2	1	0	4
Other senior civil servants[1]	51	4	1	4	6	0	15
Magistrates, professors	13	0	0	0	0	0	0
Other civil servants[2]	10	0	0	1	2	0	3
Totals	175	16	6	33	29	3	87

a. Number of individuals in occupational category
b. Holding posts in public sector
c. Public sector followed by private sector
d. Private sector
e. Holding political post only
f. Private sector followed by political post
g. Total number of individuals expanding sphere of influence
1. Civil administrators, economic planners and officials, representatives to international organizations, etc.
2. Clerks, labor inspectors, SNCF, customs officers, etc.

the politicians over matters of policy. The different outlooks of the two groups may be seen in the fact that under the Fourth Republic the politicians sought favors from the PME,* which aroused suspicion among the senior civil servants, who preferred to work with the CNPF.[23] Indeed, politicians were subjected to pressure from special interests on all sides, often boasting representatives among the deputies themselves; these pressure groups sought to initiate or block passage of bills in the legislature. From cognac distillers to tobacco planters, from small-business lobbyists to proponents of subsidies for

*The PME represented small and medium business, the CNPF big business.— Trans.

private (Catholic) schools or physicians, a long list of pressure groups thus managed to influence the politicians by reminding them of their obligations to the voters.[24]

The interests of big business were scarcely defended by politicians still largely cut off from business circles and not sharing their views; as a result, big business tended to take its problems directly to the bureaucracy, where senior officials often shared the concerns of businessmen. Like the industrialists, these officials were interested in hastening modernization of the industrial plant and hence in fostering concentration of large firms, which particularly affected the PME. The interests of small businessmen, on the other hand, were looked after by the politicians.[25]

The distance that grew up as a result between the politicians and the senior bureaucrats was a cause of deep-seated tensions and dysfunctions, which impaired government action and made it incoherent: the separation of powers gave rise to different strategies, laying bare opposing interests and conceptions. With France at that time in the thick of major industrial change, and big business trying to work toward greater concentration and higher productivity, traditional politicians were responsive instead to the imperatives of universal suffrage: mainly concerned with local demands, they tried to satisfy one by one the various special-interest groups, each of which represented so many potential voters. All-powerful under the terms of the constitution, the parliament and the government that issued from its midst acted in a disorderly fashion in response to divergent imperatives. Politicians heeded the demands of reactionary business groups, for instance, but at the same time set up a planning apparatus to accelerate and lay down guidelines for industrialization: it was the job of the officials in charge of the *commissariat général du Plan,* for example, to put their notions of economic rationality into practice. But the distance that grew up between the politicians and the senior bureaucrats made it almost impossible to formulate a coherent policy. The separation of powers survived: with the advent of the Fifth Republic, however, it would give way to a new form of integration of political and administrative power. The "Republic of deputies" was destined to be supplanted by the "Republic of functionaries."

4 The Republic of Functionaries
Toward a New Integration of Politics and the Bureaucracy

The birth of the Fifth Republic marks the downfall of the traditional professional politician, the representative of the newly ascendant strata of society, who had gradually moved into the limelight beginning with the Third Republic and the organization of large-scale political parties adept at winning elections. The governmental instability that became apparent under the Fourth Republic was due as much to the "revels" of the parties whose leaders came to power one by one as to the exclusion from power, whether by choice or by necessity, of the PC and RPC. The permanent political agitation in which the party professionals indulged made it difficult to formulate long-range programs and heightened the suspicion of the senior civil servants, who took little or no part in political life during the Third and Fourth Republics.

At first sight the political system of the Fifth Republic would seem to be the opposite of the Assembly-dominated regime: the 1958 Constitution aims deliberately to strengthen the executive at the expense of parliament. There is no need here to undertake an analysis of the Constitution itself: we need only point out that the 1958 text provides for the preeminence of the executive and frees the government from dependence on parliament, the president of the Republic becoming the principal figure in the political system: he carries out his duties with the assistance of the government, which he has the power to dismiss even if the government retains the confidence of the Assembly. Furthermore, owing to the new emphasis on "rule-making" as opposed to "law-making," the executive enjoys even greater freedom of action; similarly, the parliament no longer has control over its own agenda and meets only for short sessions, and its real role is diminished even further by new rules of procedure as well as by a weakening of the power of legislative committees. Above all, the new Constitution forbids the holding of ministerial office and of a seat in parliament at the same time: ministers must give up, at least temporarily, their seats as deputies when they are named to serve in the government. Though in actuality ways are often found to circumvent this provision, it has nevertheless played a part in putting an end to the old unity of politicians as a group: more and more they are losing the homogeneity they once had under the Third and Fourth Republics.

As specified under the terms of the Constitution, then, the government and the parliament have grown apart. Similarly, the election of the president of the Republic has from 1962 on enhanced the legitimacy of the executive, who now shares with parliament the sanction of universal suffrage. No longer is the president designated by parliament; rather, he is chosen directly by the people, the parliament having relinquished yet another chunk of its former powers. In point of fact, General de Gaulle replaced René Coty as president: a man who aimed to stand above the parties and who in his speech at Bayeux called for an end to the party system that had grown steadily stronger throughout the Fourth Republic replaced a man who was the very embodiment of the professional politician created by that system and whose whole career had been based on his strong local roots. The change of president in itself symbolized the profound transformation that the political system would undergo, a transformation reflected in the irreversible downfall of the traditional politician.

The Increasing Professionalization of the Deputies

The weakening of parliament and the considerable strengthening of the executive gave rise to a political system of a new type, long desired in France, particularly by right-wing theoreticians. As Nicholas Wahl has observed, reform committees had been set up between the wars for the purpose of doing away with the "Republic of cronies" that worked its will through parliament.[1] Under the Fourth Republic, too, the RPF had fought against the Assembly-dominated regime. In both cases the aim was to establish a regime with a strong executive who would encourage economic expansion, relying on the bureaucracy and downgrading the power of the politicians, who, it was claimed, cared only about keeping themselves in office.

The eclipse of the deputies went hand in hand with a noticeable change in their social background. Table 4.1 shows a rapid fall in the number of blue- and white-collar workers, farmers, and elementary teachers, readily explicable as the result of a series of defeats of the left in legislative elections. The declining representation of disadvantaged social groups profited the middle classes and liberal professions on the one hand, industrialists and senior civil servants on the other. Ever since the Third Republic the former group had played a prominent role in parliament, and had furnished the government with a good many ministers as well. In those days the government had been socially homogeneous, and this could not but enhance the politicians' identity as a group distinct from the social and business elites. Under the Fifth Republic the middle classes and liberal professions further increased their representation, the percentages of doctors and middle-management personnel rising to as much as double what they had been. If we look, for example, at the professional background of deputies elected during the Fifth Republic (table 4.1), we find this group accounting for 51.4 percent (including professors, journalists, doctors, lawyers, other liberal professions, engineers, middle management, military officers, and clergymen). If we add the elementary teachers and low-level civil servants, the figure rises to 59 percent. The corresponding figure for the Fourth Republic was only 51.9 percent: a considerable change, then, reflecting the changing role of parliament.

Also worthy of note is the rapid growth in the representation of two social groups quite different from the foregoing group, industrialists and senior civil servants. Between the Fourth and the Fifth Republics industrialists almost doubled their representation, and senior bureaucrats tripled theirs. This was the exact reverse of what happened to the blue- and white-collar workers: the former lost half their representatives, the latter two-thirds of theirs. These sweeping changes are clearly connected with the failure of the left to win elections after 1958.* Beyond this failure, however, it may be

━━━━━━
*Until 1981 at any rate.—Trans.

TABLE 4.1 Professional Background of French Deputies in the Fifth Republic (in %)

Years	Blue-collar workers	White-collar workers	Civil servants	Farmers	Elementary teachers	Secondary and college teachers	Journalists	Doctors	Lawyers	Liberal professions	Senior civil servants	Engineers	Middle management	Merchants	Industrialists	Military officers, clergy	Miscellaneous
1945–1958	11.9	6.3	2.7	12	5.9	8.9	5.7	5.8	12.7		3.7	4.8	3.8	5.7	6.1	1.6	1.4
1958	1.5	2.6	2.6	11	2.1	7.7	4.9	12	15.9		7.9	6	7	4.7	10.7	1.5	0.5
1962	5.1	3.6	4.5	9	3.6	6.2	4	12	11.1		8.8	4.3	9	5.3	9.2	2.7	0.8
1967	4.3	4.9	5.1	8.8	5.9	8.6	3.8	6.3	9.6	3.2	6.1	3.2	10.2	5.7	4.5	0.7	3.8
1968	2.4	1.6	6.5	7.4	1.6	6.5	3.7	14.3	10	4.9	7.1	3.2	5.3	6.3	10	1	7.1
1973	4.8	3.3	2.9	5.2	3.5	10.1	2.9	12	8	7.6	11.4	3.5	5	2.8	11.4	0.4	4.4
1958–1973	3.6	3.2	4.3	8.2	3.3	7.8	3.8	11.3	10.9	3.1	9	5	8	6.1	10.5	1.5	3.6
Active population, 1973	37.2	16.3		10.4					6.4				12.6[a]	9.5		7.6	
Occupational distribution weighted by non-PC deputies in 1973 (%)																	
1973	—	0.7	3.2	5.5	2.2	10.2	3.2	14	9.5	10	13.5	3.7	4.2	2.8	13.5	1	4.5

Taken from Véronique Aubert, "Etude sur le personnel politique français" (Thesis, University of Paris V, 1973).
[a] This figure combines the categories of middle management, elementary teachers, and civil servants.

asked whether the changes in the social structure that favored the middle classes have not contributed to the decline of parliament embodied in the 1958 Constitution. Indeed, it is likely that, formerly, working-class deputies, both white- and blue-collar, had noticeably fewer personal connections with potential voters than did members of the middle classes and the liberal professions; as members of organized political parties rather than individuals with their own private connections, these working-class deputies may have had an easier time getting into office in the past. Today, by contrast, deputies subscribing to the majority are either local figures who owe their election to their professional connections or else in many cases are unknowns elected because of their support for the majority and willingness from the outset to accept a strong executive over which they exert little influence, being indebted to the power of the executive for their own selection. In either case these deputies probably have a hard time carrying out their legislative functions.

This leads us to question some of the results obtained by Roland Cayrol, Jean-Luc Parodi, and Colette Ysmal in their book *Le Député français*. According to these authors, "the proportion of deputies belonging to 'ruling-class groups' has been increasing with each legislative election";[2] this increase, they say, has come at the expense of farmers and of the middle and "popular" classes. However, these results take on a quite different significance when we look at the occupations included in the categories to which the authors refer as "ruling-class groups" and the "middle class."[3] As they see it, ruling-class groups include industrialists, wholesalers, professionals, engineers, military officers, and high-school and university teachers. This categorization may seem somewhat heterogeneous: there is no reason why professionals, engineers, officers (whose rank is unspecified), and high-school teachers should explicitly be considered part of the ruling class in virtue of the nature of their work. These groups have no great wealth, own no means of production, and have no power; at best they may boast in some cases of a certain prestige. Hence they may be classed as members of "the middle class and liberal professions."[4]

Just as under the Third and Fourth Republics, then, deputies in the Fifth Republic have by and large not been members of the ruling class. As Olgierd Lewandowski has rightly observed, "we can understand the relations between the deputies and the leading figures of the various sectors of society (and *a fortiori* with corporate executives and cabinet assistants) only by abstracting from the fact that in general the deputies are far less well-equipped than their would-be interlocutors with the various economic, social, and cultural advantages to be had from a privileged background, Parisian upbringing, and advanced education."[5]

If we classify the professional backgrounds of the 1969-70 deputies as indicated above,[6] we find that the group made up of skilled craftsmen, lawyers, doctors, veterinarians, pharmacists, other professionals, engineers, officers, secondary and elementary teachers, journalists, technicians, middle management personnel in both public and private sectors, and other similar categories accounted for 48.5 percent of the UDR deputies, 46 percent of the RI, and 50 percent of all deputies across the board politically. Also worthy of note is the fact that in 1969[7] senior civil servants constituted the largest homogeneous group within the UDR (14 percent) and the RI (17 percent), as well as among all deputies (14 percent). In other words, deputies are mainly middle-class or professional men, men usually with local influence but more often than not no national role that could enhance the prestige of parliamentary office; there is also, however, a contingent of senior bureaucrats who enjoy a source of power unconnected with their seats in the Assembly, for whom parliament serves merely as a way station on the road to a ministry or as an emolument for ministerial service. While the old-style politicians have managed to obtain an even greater share of the seats in parliament than before, senior bureaucrats have tripled their representation as compared with their share in the Fourth Republic and have come to figure as trespassers posing a threat within parliament itself to the predominance of the professional politicians. As under the Fourth Republic, senior civil servants are especially numerous in the parties of the right; unlike in the Fourth Republic, however, now these parties are constantly in power, whereas formerly they were more often than not in opposition. This change has inevitably enhanced the influence of these senior bureaucrats even further.

Another point to notice is that while the representation of the professions and middle classes has increased significantly, deputies from these groups are distributed in a highly unequal way among the different political groupings. Looking, for example, at deputies elected in 1968, we find that "*lycée* and elementary-school teachers" make up 44 percent of the Socialist (PS) delegation in the Assembly, but only 4 percent of the UDR and 2 percent of the RI. The "Republic of teachers" is as dead as a doornail. By contrast, the "Republic of lawyers and doctors" is still potent locally to some degree, but in the national arena it must contend with the "Republic of functionaries."

Finally, it may be added that certain "apolitical" tendencies among the deputies of the majority inevitably have the effect of reinforcing the role of these deputies as local notables uninterested in national political life. The authors of *Le Député français*, for example, have drawn the conclusion that "UDR deputies on the whole come from relatively unpoliticized environments,"[8] a conclusion based on a survey of how many deputies were sons of men who belonged to political groups and who "talked politics" in an explicit way at home. Unfortunately, this highly schematic conception of politics takes no account of other, more powerful mechanisms of political socialization, which can produce a "political vision" even if "talking politics" is not a part of the daily routine.[9] Still, the observation does highlight the fact that, for the deputies of the majority, party affiliation is relatively unimportant. This relative indifference to party, which stands in sharp contrast to the more or less unwavering political commitment and consciousness of the families of left-wing deputies, inevitably induces the deputies of the majority to refrain from putting forth any specific political program of their own, encouraging them instead to place their trust in the executive, on whose influence they are dependent for reelection. Ultimately the power of parliament itself cannot but be impaired by this tendency.

Civil-Service Ministers

Since the inception of the Fifth Republic, the socioprofessional makeup of the government has ceased to mirror that of parliament. Table 4.2 is basic, we think, to an understanding of the changes in parliament and the executive branch. While the middle classes and professionals made rapid progress in gaining parliamentary seats, they lost considerable ground in the government. Ministers who were once lawyers, for example, are only one-third as common in the Fifth Republic as in the Fourth. The number of doctors, journalists, and middle management personnel in governments of the Fifth Republic also fell. Teachers from elementary schools have vanished entirely. The series of defeats sustained by the parties of the left, together with the creation of a party of a new type, which has been in power constantly since 1958, has thus led to a significant decline of the professional politician.

The trend in the government is thus the reverse of what has taken place in parliament. More and more Assembly seats have been won by professionals and members of the middle classes: most of them have managed to use their network of personal contacts to cope with the local demands made on them, while relinquishing any active role in the legislative process, as they are encouraged to do by the 1958 Constitution and even more by the way its provisions are put into practice. In the government, on the other hand, their representation has been declining steadily.

Now, as we have seen, a second group has also increased its numbers in parliament, though its share of seats is significantly less, namely, the group of senior civil servants. They amount to only a small minority within the Assembly as a whole. In the government, however, we find three times as many senior civil servants as under the Fourth Republic. This fact we regard as basic: although senior bureaucrats account for only 9 percent of the deputies in the Assembly, they occupy 29.7 percent of the posts in the government under the Fifth Republic, compared with 11.8 percent under the Fourth. By themselves they fill almost a third of the top spots in the Fifth Republic. They have been the beneficiaries of the gradual withdrawal of doctors, lawyers, and the like from the executive branch: thus little by little they are replacing the professional politicians.

One final point to notice in table 4.2 is the continuing standstill of big representatives of business, who even under the

TABLE 4.2 Professional Background of Ministers and Secretaries of State Under the Fourth and Fifth Republics

		Farm workers	Farmers	Blue-collar workers	White-collar workers, middle management	Elementary teachers	Secondary and college teachers	Lawyers, judges	Journalists	Doctors, veterinarians, pharmacists	Liberal professions, top management	Senior civil servants	Engineers	Craftsmen, merchants	Industrialists	Military officers	Miscellaneous, or no information	Total
1944 to 58	N	1	10	7	2	10	24	53	19	15	2	27	13	6	31	4	3	227
	%	0.4	4.4	3	0.8	4.4	10.6	23.3	8.3	6.6	0.9	11.8	5.7	2.6	14	1.7	1.3	
1958 to 69	N	0	1	0	0	1	17	10	6	2	4	23	4	1	15	2	0	86
	%	0	1.1	0	0	1.1	19.7	11.8	6.9	2.3	4.6	26.7	4.6	1.1	17.4	2.3	0	
1969 to 74	N	0	1	0	0	0	6	6	1	4	9	26	2	2	9	0	1	67
	%	0	1.6	0	0	0	8.9	8.9	1.6	5.9	13.4	38.8	2.9	2.9	13.4	0	1.6	
1974 to Jan. 75	N	0	0	1	1	0	4	1	3	3	0	13	1	1	6	0	2	37
	%	0	0	2.7	2.7	0	10	2.7	8.1	8.1	0	35	2.7	2.7	16	0	5.4	
1958 to 75	N	0	2	1	1	1	24	14	9	8	10	45	5	2	25	2	3	152
	%	0	1.6	0.6	0.6	0.8	15.8	9.2	5.9	5.2	6.5	29.7	3.3	1.2	16.5	1.2	1.9	

Sources: 1944-67: E.G. Lewis, "Social Backgrounds of French Ministers," *The Western Political Quarterly* (September 1970):567. *Who's Who in France?* (1967-75).

Fifth Republic have not, for the time being anyway, moved into government: their share of posts hardly changes from one republic to the next. The full significance of this observation emerges when we compare it with the steadily increasing prominence of the senior civil servants. The essential point is this: traditional political professionals have been expelled from the precincts of power, but the commanding heights of government remain inaccessible to intruders from the world of big business. In this way the distinctive identity of the state has been preserved in an attempt to reconcile two different types of professionalization, which earlier had clashed: in parliament, the old-style political professional; in the government, senior civil servants drawn largely from the Grands Corps, men with an expertise profoundly different in nature from that of the deputies.

A further consequence of this deep-seated division is that the deputies have tended more and more to rely on their local power bases, sinking their roots deeper in an effort to hold on to a part of their power. Thus we may note that whereas only 28 percent of the deputies were also members of the *conseils généraux* in 1946, that figure had risen to 44 percent by 1962.[10] More generally, the fraction of deputies holding local elective office of any kind rose from 63 percent in 1958 to 79.4 percent in 1967.[11] We even find a fair number of cases in which the classic career trajectory is reversed, a deputy winning local office after having been elected to parliament. Deputies, then, have been concentrating increasingly on their own districts, going so far as to hand over to the ministers certain local offices of national importance, such as chairmanships of the *conseils régionaux*.[12]

In this way a certain division of labor has grown up between the parliament and the government: a game has begun from which big business has been excluded, at least as far as holding office is concerned. Parliament has taken on the job of administering local politics, while the government has taken over management of national politics.[13] This split has been accentuated by the fact that in many cases ministers are chosen from outside parliament: it is becoming more and more common, as we shall see later on, for the call to a ministry to follow a stint as a high official in the administration; only later does the former minister run for a seat as a deputy.

This inevitably affects the nature of the deputy's role, since his influence depends on the way power is distributed: important business interests will take their case directly to government ministers and senior bureaucrats, bypassing the deputies and thereby significantly diminishing their role.[14] Similarly, at the local level, the bilateral relationship that has been said to grow up between the prefect and "his" notables[15] tends to leave the deputies out in the cold, since the prefect will deal directly with the leading business interests in his region or *département*.

Accordingly, deputies will tend to find their influence sought out only in connection with strictly local matters, in keeping with their position, thus effectively excluding them from participation in affairs of great moment. The deputy is reduced to little more than a "ward heeler" from whom favors are sought in dealing with run-of-the-mill problems. A study of the mail received by deputies has shown that they are no longer regarded as influential figures in the national arena,[16] and that they have lost the image they had under the Third and Fourth Republics. The division of labor established by the 1958 Constitution has thus led to a downgrading of parliamentary office in the minds of the voters, who more and more see themselves as represented by the executive.[17] No longer is the parliament under the Fifth Republic considered, as Alain once said of earlier parliaments, "a power in the region to make the prefect quake in his boots." On the contrary, parliament has increasingly given way before the power of the executive in every area; the executive claims to govern the social system as a whole, and consequently it exercises greater political and bureaucratic influence.

The Professional Development of Former Members of Parliament

We have done research on the Fifth Republic similar to the study whose results were described in the previous chapter. This time our sample consisted of 190 former members of parliament, 27 senators and 163 deputies. The latter held seats in three different legislatures: 1962-67, 1967-68, 1968-73. The senators in the sample were those who failed to win reelection in the 1965, 1968, and 1971 by-elections. Deputies and senators were chosen for inclusion in our study on the basis of their answers to questionnaires sent out to a total of 450 members who had failed to be reelected.

The percentage of ex-members gaining seats on the boards of directors of national firms is even smaller than under the Fourth Republic: only 6.8 percent of our sample. This figure confirms that the distance between parliament and the major centers of economic decision-making has increased. As under the Fourth Republic, the party label seems to be a very significant variable in determing whether or not a former member of parliament obtains a seat on the board of a large firm, the mere fact of holding office not being decisive in itself. Board seats went almost exclusively to supporters of the majority. This suggests that the ties between business and politics are formed before the politician wins election, the game being played out at the party level. Thus the mere fact of holding office in parliament has relatively little effect. Then, too, just as under the Fourth Republic, most of the board seats went to senior bureaucrats who had also sat in parliament: once again, the business contacts that go along with their jobs are far more important than their seats in parliament in helping them to launch careers in business.

By way of contrast, participation in the management of local firms and agencies by former members of parliament is an important phenomenon under the Fifth Republic (we find 58 instances in our sample), just as it was earlier under the Fourth Republic. About a third of the members turned out of office obtained such posts, and very likely this figure errs on the low side. Just as under the Fourth Republic, access to such positions seems to be strongly correlated with membership in parliament. Indeed, the percentage of ex-members obtaining jobs of this kind increases with the length of term in office: of the 58 individuals who got these posts, only 6 had been in parliament for less than five years. Experience in parliament and the prestige of the job, then, seem to have played an important role in this respect.

What is more, here we find a rather equitable distribution of the available jobs among the various political groupings, as opposed to the situation that exists, as we have seen, with respect to larger firms: 22 former members from the majority, 20 from the center opposition, and 16 from the left managed to get these posts after leaving office. This improved balance confirms that on the local level it is the fact of having served in parliament in itself that is taken into account, even above party affiliation. Furthermore, the socioprofessional background of these ex-members, under Fourth and Fifth Republic alike, differs sharply from that of ex-members who obtained seats on the boards of large firms; we find 18 farmers, 17 professionals, 6 elementary school teachers, 5 company officials, 4 senior functionaries, 3 middle-level managers from the private sector, 3 junior functionaries, 1 merchant, and 1 officer. This distribution is indicative of the local influence exerted by many former members of parliament, whose occupations bring them into almost daily contact with a segment of the voting population, thus fostering strong local roots.

As under the Fourth Republic, former members of parliament have found their way into jobs with local agencies, which they serve by providing liaison with the central government. Under the Fifth Republic 78 percent of the posts obtained by former members are with local public or semipublic agencies (housing authorities, development committees, and so forth), the remainder being with private concerns, such as agricultural cooperatives. Under the Fifth Republic, then, the ex-member wields a certain influence on the local level, but he has little contact with big business.

As we did earlier in the case of the Fourth Republic, we have tried to measure the job mobility of former members of parliament in the Fifth Republic. The results are quite similar: once again, two-thirds of the former members did not profit professionally in any way from their stint in office. Mainly it is the petty functionaries and elementary school teachers who improve their professional status or take up political careers. More interesting, however, is the fact that the most striking phenomenon in the Fourth Republic, the accelerated career advancement of senior functionaries, is still more pronounced under the Fifth, during which 59 percent of senior bureaucrats elected to parliament managed to gain professionally from their term in office (compared with 50 percent under the Fourth Republic). Thus the senior civil servants, who since 1958 have dominated the executive, have found that going into parliament offers considerable advantages. As we shall see next, these advantages come not only from a stint in parliament but also from service in the government of the "Republic of functionaries."

The Professional Development of Former Ministers

Under the Fifth Republic the government is not required to reflect the composition of parliament. This divergence is facilitated by the fact that the government can count almost automatically on the support of a majority of the members of parliament, who are dependent on it for their reelection. The incompatibility between holding office in the government and holding a seat in parliament established by article 23 of the 1958 Constitution has led to a diversification of personnel in the two branches, a development also encouraged by the fact that many ministers come to the government directly from the ranks of the senior civil service without first passing through parliament, though ultimately they do usually seek a parliamentary mandate.

These differences between the parliament and the government emerge clearly when we look at the professional development of former ministers of the Fifth Republic. Whereas members of parliament turned out of office in the Fifth Republic had careers similar to those of their counterparts in the Fourth Republic, the subsequent careers of former ministers differ profoundly from one era to the next. This time our sample consists of 85 ministers and secretaries of state who left the government, even if only temporarily, before May 1974. Unlike ministers of the Fourth Republic, those of the Fifth quickly obtained seats on boards of directors of national firms (see table 4.3).

The figure of 32.8 percent in table 4.3 is of limited significance: some ministers left the government and almost immediately returned to seats in parliament as either senators or deputies (whether because the government was reshuffled after legislative elections or because the ministers could regain their old seats thanks to timely resignations by their replacements). Furthermore, some ministers were mayors of large cities and thus continued to hold important political posts after leaving the government.

TABLE 4.3   Participation of Ministers on Boards of Directors (%)

	Fourth Republic	Fifth Republic
No participation	78	55.2
Continued in seat held beforehand	3.9	8.2
Acquired seat after leaving office	13.5[a]	32.8
Unclassifiable	4.5	3.5

[a] This figure represents only those ministers who obtained seats during the Fourth Republic, and does not include any who may have acquired a seat after 1958.

For these reasons, it is a good idea to distinguish two categories of former ministers: first, those who remain fully involved in political life, and second, those who are obliged to quit politics—whether temporarily or permanently, voluntarily or involuntarily—after leaving the government. Statistical analysis of the 37 ministers of the Fifth Republic who left political life for six months or more yields the following figures: 40 percent did not serve on any board of directors; 5.5 percent continued in board seats acquired before election; 54 percent obtained board seats after leaving office.

Thus more than half of the ministers of the Fifth Republic who left active political life, even temporarily, acquired seats on the boards of directors of public or private business organizations.

Another difference between the Fourth and Fifth Republics should be noted: under the Fourth, whether or not a former minister obtained a board seat depended mainly on his party affiliation. Since this distribution worked against the left and the center-left and gave a very marked advantage to the RPF, it was possible to deduce that contacts between the worlds of politics and business were above all a partisan phenomenon.

Under the Fifth Republic, the breakdown by party is less significant, perhaps because of the more restricted range of participation in the government. Table 4.4, however, suggests that ministers belonging to the UDR and "unaffiliated" ministers (actually senior functionaries brought into the government under the aegis of the majority) had an easier time obtaining board seats in the business world.[18] We may conclude,

TABLE 4.4. Party Affiliation and Participation in Boards of Directors under the Fifth Republic (%)

	UDR	RI	Center	No party affiliation[1]
No participation	51	66.6	53.3	45.5
Seat held beforehand	7.5	16.6	13.3	----
Seat obtained after leaving office	41.5	----	26.6	45.5
Unclassifiable	----	16.6	6.6	9

1. All senior civil servants.

then, that the switch from government to business is most clearly and prominently associated with the party that has been at the center of the political system since 1958, namely, the UDR. The ease with which senior civil servants have moved since that date from government into business (whether in the public or the private sector) attests to the strong ties that have bound the machinery of government to civil society under the Fifth Republic. As we shall see later on, the explanation lies with the role of the ENA and the attempt to have the state take control of the social environment, an attempt implicit in the Gaullist program. The closer ties between government and business would seem to be a consequence of the strengthening of the executive, which has helped bring the business world closer to people in the government; this may be contrasted with the situation under the Third and Fourth Republics, during which businessmen brought pressure to bear only on the bureaucracy and not on members of the government as such, much less on members of parliament, with whom businessmen had few direct contacts owing to the peculiar professional backgrounds, described earlier, of the politicians. Government-business links also date from the arrival in power of political forces closely connected with the business world: the 39 percent figure "scored" by the RPF during the Fourth Republic in a sense anticipates the 41 percent achieved by the UDR during the Fifth. As further support for this hypothesis, notice that during the Fourth Republic the occupational makeup of the RPF parliamentary contingent was already rather distinctive: company officials, senior functionaries, and military officers were overrepresented, these three categories (close to the triad described by C. Wright Mills) accounting for more than 40 percent of our sample. Finally, we may look into the professional backgrounds of men who left the government and subsequently obtained board seats, some 13.5 percent of all ex-members of the government in the sample firm under Fourth Republic (24 individuals in all) and 32.8 percent from the Fifth (28 individuals) (see table 4.3).

TABLE 4.5   Professional Background of Government Officials Obtaining Board Seats after Leaving Office (%)

Professional background	Fourth Republic	Fifth Republic
Senior civil servants	24	35.7
Corporate officers in industry or commerce	20.8	28.5
Management, private sector	4.2	7.2
Liberal professions	4.2	7.2
Military officers	8.3	----
Academics	8.3	----
Professional politicians (deputies, senators, mayors, etc.)	17.7	21.4
Officials of Public-employee unions	12.5	----

It is striking to note once again how much senior bureaucrats and industrialists, many more of whom served in governments under the Fifth Republic than under the Fourth, profited from their terms as ministers. Conversely, professional politicians, along with union officials, constitute a group that has no equivalent under the Fifth Republic: they profited to some extent from their service in the government, though they were estranged from the world of business at the outset.

The changeover to the business sector, then, involved a larger number of ministers under the Fifth Republic and concerned individuals having a specific political orientation. Next, we must investigate the nature of the tie to the business community and give further details about the sectors involved.

To begin with, we may note that the breakdown between the public and the private sector remained quite stable from the Fourth to the Fifth Republic. Under the former, 12 out of 24 ministers went into public-sector jobs, 8 into the private sector, and 4 into both. Under the Fifth Republic we find identical proportions: out of 28 individuals in all, 14 went into the public sector, 11 into the private, and 3 into both.

However, the phenomenon seems to have become more formalized under the Fifth Republic. In the first place, each individual involved holds a greater number of posts on the average (1.8 in the public sector under the Fifth Republic as against 1.1 under the Fourth; 2.6 in the private sector under the Fifth as against 2.2 under the Fourth). The formalization of the transfer from government to business may be seen even more clearly when we look at the qualitative aspect: under the Fifth Republic 65 percent of the public-sector firms in which ex-ministers became involved were concerned with regional development work. Among other examples, we may mention the boards of directors of the port authorities of Rouen, Paris, and Marseilles; the Mont Blanc tunnels; the Fréjus highway tunnel; the development of the old market district of Paris, Les Halles; the investment group that financed development of the Fos region; and the financial and technical agency responsible for the Paris region. Other public-sector enterprises were occasionally represented: a bank, Air France, Elf, and Radio Monte-Carlo,* for example. This formalized interchange underscores the extreme politicization of regional development in France, which has in part conditioned the political process in the regions and *départements:* it has helped the government to control the fundamental social processes and greatly influenced campaign strategies. For instance, the government has been able in this way to establish close ties with socioprofessional groups whose interests are bound up with regional development plans. We offer this suggestion now as a hypothesis, but we shall see later on that it is supported by the fact that a great many prefects have taken jobs in various businesses connected in one way or another with regional development, businesses in which,

---

*State-owned airline, oil company, and radio station, respectively.—Trans.

like ex-ministers, they play a predominantly political role. Under the Fourth Republic, by way of contrast, regional development played a less important part, though even then nearly 40 percent of the public-sector enterprises involved (the port authority of Nantes and the planning commission for the English Channel bridge, for example) had something to do with this kind of activity.

Private-sector firms with which former ministers of the Fifth Republic accepted jobs do not really share any common characteristics: it should be noted, however, that they were often very large companies (Rhône-Poulenc, Peugeot, Pechiney, Denain, Ciment Lafargue, Compagnie française des pétroles, La Paternelle, Bouygues, and so on). Under the Fourth Republic, ministers took jobs with more regionally oriented firms (Société industrielle et financière d'Artois, Forges de Strasbourg, and the like), or with firms operating in the colonies (Caoutchouc du Mekong, Société mauritanienne de navigation, Compagnie française de charbonnage de Dakar, and so forth). To sum up, then, large numbers of former ministers of the Fifth Republic, particularly senior civil servants who had moved into the government, took jobs in the private sector, frequently with very large firms, firms that had not welcomed ex-ministers before the establishment of the Gaullist political system. By such means have the ties between the executive and the business world been strengthened, in public and private sector alike.

To complete this line of argument, let us take a look at the professional development of former ministers of the Fifth Republic, as we have already done for the Fourth. Notice to begin with that the former exhibit far greater upward mobility than the latter. Indeed, during the Fourth Republic only 8.9 percent of former ministers moved to "higher-status professions," as compared with 19 percent during the Fifth. Another difference is that under the Fifth Republic former ministers who did move up in the status hierarchy were often senior civil servants who obtained important jobs in the public or semipublic sector after leaving the government. The observation made earlier about bureaucrats who had moved into parliamentary seats is thus confirmed: since 1958 the exchange of personnel between the world of politics and the upper bureaucracy has become more and more formalized and increasingly bilateral.[19]

Under the Fifth Republic, then, it would seem that the governmental sphere was in closer communication with the upper reaches of the bureaucracy than with political life and the political parties in the classical sense. In any case this was clearly the trend of events: ever more upwardly mobile ex-ministers moved into careers in the business world, whether in firms tied to the state or in private-sector companies. Cut off from traditional politicians, who were drawn mainly from the middle classes and the professions, government ministers of the new stripe, particularly the senior bureaucrats among them, who constituted the most homogeneous group within the government and who enjoyed ever-increasing autonomy in recruiting into their own ranks, attempted to establish close contacts with the world of business. From this standpoint the changes in the professional qualifications of members of the government can be seen as part of a process that encouraged the formation of close ties between business and government. Apparently, a new unity within the apparatus of government went hand in hand with a desire on the part of the state to extend its control to vital sectors of society as a whole, in order to strengthen its own capacity to act and to enhance its independence.

5   The Growing Autonomy of
     Government and Bureaucracy
     under the Fifth Republic

The key feature of government under the Fifth Republic seems to be the control exerted by the bureaucracy over the executive. Not only are nearly a third of the ministers drawn from the upper reaches of the civil service, but approximately the same number are also children of bureaucrats.[1] Thus the effect has been to consolidate the power of families that have served the state generation after generation. Ministers drawn from the bureaucracy subscribe to the principles of meritocracy, by which their power is legitimated and their competence certified. Nearly half the ministers of the Fifth Republic have passed such difficult competitive examinations as the *agrégation* for admission to secondary-school or university-level teaching posts, the entrance exam for the ENA or the Ecole Polytechnique, and the like; the "Republic of clever students"[2] is a reality. The technocratic professionalism of the senior bureaucrats who define the general interest as they understand it[3] has taken precedence over the political professionalism of the traditional politician.

The Functional Specialization of the Machinery of Government: the Grands Corps, the Ministerial Staffs, and the Semi-public Sector

The ministers of the Fifth Republic have merely been following the example set by their prime ministers: all the prime ministers of the Fifth Republic* have in fact been top-grade civil servants. Maurice Couve de Murville and Jacques Chaban-Delmas were Inspecteurs des Finances, Michel Debré and Georges Pompidou were members of the Conseil d'Etat, Pierre Messmer was governor of France's overseas territories, and

---
*Before Raymond Barre.—Trans.

Jacques Chirac was a member of the Cour des comptes. Many ministers of the Fifth Republic had no party affiliation before becoming members of the government: rather, they respected a "mandarin" logic, as Matei Dogan has put it. Specifically, out of 128 ministers (including the ministers of the Chirac government), 56 followed the buraucratic route: 39 first served on a minister's staff, then became deputies (in most cases being "parachuted" into a safe seat), and finally ministers themselves, while 17 went directly from a ministerial staff position to a ministerial appointment.[4]

It is an undeniable fact that if one looks, for example, at the careers of ministers drawn from the senior civil service under the presidency of General de Gaulle, who of course made no secret of his wish to govern above the parties, one finds that virtually none of them was a deputy before becoming a minister; moreover, relatively few became deputies after leaving their ministerial posts. For example, W. Baumgartner, B. Chenot, P. Guillaumat, P. Chatenet, and L. Paye are all senior bureaucrats who were not deputies before becoming ministers and did not run for seats in the Assembly afterwards; similarly, M. Couve de Murville, L. Joxe, and P. Messmer are senior bureaucrats who held no seat in parliament before 1967–68.

If, nevertheless, the vast majority of ministers of the Fifth Republic did hold seats in parliament before entering the government, nearly 40 percent of the future ministers took cabinet staff positions shortly before obtaining their portfolios.[5] In other words, the most common route to a minister's seat in the Fifth Republic has been by way of the ministerial staffs, which are of course overwhelmingly composed of senior civil servants: the grip of the top bureaucrats on policy at the highest levels can only have been strengthened by this process. Inevitably, too, it has still further weakened the power of the professional politicians, who usually begin by being elected to local office before embarking on careers quite different from those of ministers, as we have seen. Once again two different modes of professionalization have come into conflict with each other, increasing the separaration between the two centers of political power (the parliament and the government).

In the Fifth Republic, the route to the ministries has changed; it now passes through the cabinet staff and from there to the government, rather than passing through parliament as in the past. In 1968, for example, more than 90 percent of the members of the ministerial staffs were drawn from the bureaucracy, largely from its top grades: 50 percent from the Grands Corps (Inspection des Finances, Conseil d'Etat, Cour des comptes, and diplomatic and prefectural corps), and another 25 percent from high-level posts in central government agencies.[6] The private sector is almost entirely excluded from the ministerial staffs, through which most future ministers pass. This mode of recruitment has greatly enhanced the autonomy of the governmental machinery, which has severed its ties with both private-interest groups and the traditional political professionals. To some extent the governmental apparatus itself has become a homogeneous unit, as a result of the increased politicization of the senior civil service: despite the technical nature of much staff work, some political loyalty is required by the ministers, men who have moved from being senior bureaucrats themselves into ministerial positions in the service of the majority.

It is worth emphasizing, moreover, that the involvement of the Grands Corps in the government has increased since the Fourth Republic: even then many staff members—though proportionally fewer than during the Fifth Republic—were drawn from the top ranks of the bureaucracy, but they had to work with ministers who were traditional politicians, whose goals and methods they did not share. This situation has been altered profoundly under the Fifth Republic: the minister and his staff have similar social backgrounds, share the same values, and are embarked on more or less identical careers. This has led to an increasing politicization of the senior civil service: while 48 percent of the prefects of the Fourth Republic served on ministerial staffs, under the Fifth Republic the comparable figure has risen to 65 percent.[7]

Notice, too, that members of the Conseil d'Etat are quite willing to accept cabinet staff posts, but practically none of them have gone into parliament. It will be recalled that under the July Monarchy a great many members of the Conseil sat in parliament; under the Fifth Republic virtually none do, the preferred choice being to seek staff positions that open the way to a minister's portfolio.[8] This shift has contributed to the growing autonomy of the governmental machinery, which is increasingly estranged from the professional politicians and yet still so specialized in its functions as to be distinct from the world of business.

TABLE 5.1   Staffs and Corps

Corps	%
Inspections des Finances	65
Conseil d'Etat	49
Cour des comptes	46
Inspections generales	40
Diplomatic corps	30
Prefectoral corps	30
Controleurs civils	24
Administrateurs civils de l'Economie et des Finances	23
Administrateurs civils[1]	8 to 15
Economic growth	11
Administrative tribunals	8

1. 8 to 15% depending on the ministry in question, excepting the staff of the prime minister, with 31% assigned.

Source: Jean-Luc Bodiguel, "Les anciens élèves de l'ENA et les cabinets ministériels," *Annuaire de la Fonction publique, 1973–1974*, p. 363. The period 1945–69 is covered.

As Jean-Luc Bodiguel has shown (table 5.1), the Grands Corps have taken the lion's share of staff posts. Now, it so happens that the students of the ENA who manage to get into the Grand Corps so as to be in a position, when the time is ripe, to move to a ministerial staff post and ultimately, if they are lucky, to a ministerial appointment, are drawn from higher social strata than the average ENA student. As Alain Darbel and Dominique Schnapper have observed, the social backgrounds of Grand Corps members who obtain staff jobs are markedly superior to the backgrounds of those who do not.[9]

To our way of thinking, however, the most significant point is that the Grands Corps members who staff the cabinets through which future ministers are likely to pass are not only particularly well-off socially but also very often children of bureaucratic officials. From 1953 to 1963, out of 253 ENA graduates in the Grands Corps, 103 were children of civil servants, 90 of whom were in the very highest civil service grades (see table 5.2). Thus slightly less than half the members of the Grands Corps were children of high-ranking civil servants. Senior civil servants who become ministers are to a large extent members of families with administrative traditions.[10]

We regard these observations as essential for evaluating the importance of the growing autonomy of the machinery of government and its separation from the traditional politicians who fill the benches of parliament. The degree to which the governmental apparatus is closed to outsiders is increased by the fact that most of the members of the Grands Corps, in many cases themselves children of senior bureaucrats, move from jobs with their own Corps either into ministerial staff

TABLE 5.2 Social Background of Members of Grands Corps and Diplomatic Corps Graduated from ENA between 1953 and 1963

Parent's profession	Conseil d'Etat	Inspection des Finances	Cour des comptes	Foreign affairs	Totals
Civil service grade A1	8	10	8	11	37
A2	14	16	12	11	53
B	1	3	4	1	9
C	—	1	1	—	2
D	—	1	1	—	2
Total	23	31	26	23	103
Craftsmen, merchants	6	12	5	4	27
Plant managers	—	5	6	5	16
Management personnel	13	14	11	10	48
White-collar workers	2	3	1	3	9
Liberal professions	9	9	11	7	36
Renters, landowners, no profession	1	1	—	—	2
Farmers (small, medium, large)	1	6	1	2	10
Blue-collar workers	2	—	—	—	2
	57	81	61	54	253

Source: Archives of the ENA.

positions—and sometimes even into the minister's chair itself—or else directly into jobs controlled by the bureaucracy or in the semipublic sector, to which they are promoted by government appointment. Almost a third of the high-ranking bureaucrats leaving staff posts under the Fifth Republic have taken this latter route.[11] For a senior functionary, then, a stint in a cabinet staff post is often a stepping-stone to quick promotion. Furthermore, staff jobs are of much greater benefit to those senior functionaries who come from elite social backgrounds and who are, in many cases, children of functionaries than they are to other bureaucrats of lower status (e.g., administrateurs civils).

These remarks apply particularly to members of the staffs of the prime minister and the president of the Republic. Senior civil servants for the most part, they constitute a very homogeneous group that has only rarely taken in individuals from the private sector. In this regard, it is worth mentioning that Georges Pompidou more than anyone else, both as prime minister and as president, opened his staff to individuals from the private sector, who accounted for 10 percent of his presidential staff, whereas no such individuals were to be found on the staffs of Debré, Couve de Murville, or Chaban-Delmas when each was prime minister. Conversely, senior civil servants, drawn both from the governmental bureaucracy and from the semipublic sector, accounted for 83.4 percent of General de Gaulle's staff, 80 percent of Couve de Murville's, 84 percent of Chaban-Delmas's, 83.7 percent of Messmer's, but only 68 percent of Pompidou's presidential staff.[12] These differences, about which we shall have more to say later on, can be seen as signs of varying ambitions to maintain a certain distance between the machinery of government and the world of business. Most pronounced in the "Gaullist" staffs, this distance, as well as its inevitable concomitant claim to state independence, was lessened considerably under Pompidou, whose staffs were more open to the business world. This reduced "independence" further manifested itself in more liberal economic policies with regard to large firms and also in a reduction of the state's efforts to plan the economy and thereby exert its control over business.

Many staff members subsequently took jobs in the semipublic sector and so continued to work within the machinery of government: 45 percent of Debré's staff, for example, went into business, 77 percent of them in the semipublic sector; similarly, 38 percent of Couve de Murville's staff took business posts, 87 percent of them in the semipublic sector. By contrast, only 24 percent of Pompidou's staff as prime minister went into business, and only 57 percent of them took jobs in the semipublic sector. Furthermore, it should be noted that many of these individuals took jobs having to do with culture or the mass media (ORTF, Sofirad, Havas), energy (Charbonnage, EGF, CEA), or banking (Crédit lyonnais, Société générale).[13]

We are now in a position to make the following observation: although access to posts in government has always been tightly controlled and closed to outsiders, there has been more openness on the "exit" side—some members of ministerial staffs, for example, have chosen to go into business afterwards, even though they came to their staff posts originally from the upper reaches of the civil service. This shift from the public to the private sector,* which we shall examine in detail later on, is already in evidence at this point in our discussion. Looking at Pompidou's presidential staff, for example, we find that 3 percent of its members who left to go into business (18 percent of the staff in all) took jobs with private firms. This flow of personnel into the private sector, more or less pronounced according to the staff (quite insignificant, for example, in the Couve de Murville, Chaban-Delmas, and Messmer cabinets), is indicative of a relatively greater degree of openness of the machinery of government to the world of business. Like the influx into the semipublic sector, the influx into private business involved mainly the cultural sphere (Hachette, Radio Monte-Carlo) or banking (Worms, Suez, etc.), that is, those areas in which it is possible to exert the most effective control over civil society or social and cultural life in general.[14] We shall return to the problem of "pantouflage" later on, treating it in more general terms. For the time being we need only note that the personnel filling top government posts exhibit a remarkable homogeneity as a result of the senior civil servants' firm grip on the apparatus of state.

---

*Referred to rather picturesquely in French as "pantouflage."—Trans.

Special Appointments to the Grands Corps, or the Difficulty of Access to the Senior Civil Service

This homogeneity is due, it would seem, to the almost complete inability of outsiders to gain access to the machinery of government. For further proof of this contention, we shall look next at special appointments to the Grands Corps, which are almost completely closed to individuals from the world of business. For the most part the Grands Corps date from the Ancien Régime and appointment to them has been based ever since their inception on political criteria: indeed, the Grands Corps have had the confidence of those in power, who have made use of the Corps to tighten their control over the machinery of government. Not until the Third Republic, for example, were *auditeurs* of the Conseil d'Etat recruited by competitive examination, and until 1900 members of the Conseil were named at the sole discretion of the president of the Republic. Hence there was no standard of advancement based on a system of rules applicable to all. Nominations were often justified on political grounds, and in any case the mode of recruitment guaranteed that the social backgrounds of auditeurs would be quite homogeneous: the *grande bourgeoisie* sent its children to the Ecole libre des sciences politiques and then used the contacts made there to get them jobs, in some cases on the Conseil d'Etat. Only after the Liberation, with the creation of the ENA and the elimination of individual entrance exams for each Grands Corps, was an attempt made to democratize recruitment. At the same time the number of places to which nomination could be made at the sole discretion of the political authorities was considerably reduced. Even today, however, a fairly significant number of such places remain in each of the Grands Corps, except the Inspection des Finances, which first allowed special appointments only recently, under the Fifth Republic.[15]

The changes in the recruitment procedure for the Conseil d'Etat are comparable to changes affecting recruitment to the Cour des comptes, which has also shifted from purely discretionary appointments often based on political considerations to an entrance exam specially tailored to the Corps and, finally, to recruitment through the ENA. Once again, however, special appointments do exist, allowing for the nomination of individuals not accepted through the normal channel, that is, via competitive examination for admission to ENA, followed by job selection based on rank in the graduating class. For this reason we felt it would be interesting to look systematically at the present situation with regard to special appointments to the Grand Corps, in order to find out whether or not political influence, elimination of which was the express purpose for creation of the ENA, continues to play a part. Are special appointments merely a way of increasing mobility within the civil service and of avoiding the danger of ossification of the Grands Corps, working against their isolation by bringing in new skills? Have they allowed the creation of a new group of senior bureaucrats less homogeneous than the old one, thereby making it harder for certain sectors of the state apparatus to acquire functional autonomy vis-à-vis the political authorities? And finally, have special appointments led to some degree of politicization of the senior civil service? In this regard it will be interesting to see how far the Gaullist conception of an independent state has been realized in the present relationship between the political authorities and the senior civil service.[16]

The Conseil d'Etat

Special appointments to the Conseil d'Etat are of two kinds: ordinary and extraordinary. Ordinary special appointments are made by the Council of Ministers, as opposed to the usual recruitment through competitive examination. Ordinary special appointees account for half the membership of the Conseil d'Etat. In effect, one-third of the council members are named directly by the Council of Ministers, while two-thirds are recruited within the corps from among the maîtres des requêtes, a quarter of whom are also special appointees, while the rest are former auditeurs. These ordinary special appointees are joined by a group of extraordinary special appointees. Usually twelve in number and nominated by the Council of Ministers for four-year nonrenewable terms, they are chosen from among "qualified individuals in various walks of life," including health, education, the military, industry, unions, and so forth. Generally selected because they have reached the pinnacle of their respective professions, these leading figures from business, the military, the bureaucracy, and social-service institutions spend the last years of their active lives as members of the Conseil d'Etat, though apparently without playing a great role in its activities. In studying special appointments, then, we must distinguish between ordinary and extraordinary appointees.

We shall next consider the professional backgrounds of the special appointees, using as sources both *Who's Who* and the *Annuaire du Conseil d'Etat,* from which we can find out the precise nature of the last post held prior to council appointment. In cases where this last post was on a ministerial staff (as with 58 percent of the maîtres des requêtes and 18 percent of the ordinary appointees to the Conseil), we shall further try to show that strictly political considerations had some influence on the appointments. These results cover all special appointees appearing in the *Annuaire du Conseil d'Etat* between 1958 and 1974: 91 ordinary special appointees (59 conseillers d'Etat, 32 maîtres des requêtes) and 50 extraordinary appointees (see table 5.3).

To begin with, note the extremely uneven distribution of occupations: the vast majority are upper-class. Only among the extraordinary special appointees do we find blue- and white-collar workers, who account for 8 percent of the total: one mechanic, one factory worker, one assistant accountant, and one draftsman, or four of the five union representatives named to the Conseil d'Etat.

Among the 91 ordinary special appointees, there is one worker, but he had served on several ministerial staffs between 1936 and 1945 before being named (after serving in the Resistance) to a special seat on the Conseil d'Etat in 1946. Mention must be made of the considerable overrepresentation of the public sector as compared with the private: 60 percent of ordinary special appointees were senior government bureaucrats, as were 30 percent of the extraordinary appointees; the corresponding figures are 9.9 percent and 12 percent, respectively, for engineers working in the public sector; 18.7 percent and 6 percent for magistrates; and, finally, 6.6 percent and 14 percent for academics.

If we look only at top-ranking bureaucrats from the administration (73 persons, 16 of them extraordinary appointees),

TABLE 5.3   Professional Background of Special Appointees to the Conseil d'Etat (%)

Professional Background	Ordinary Special Appointments	Extraordinary Special Appointments
Blue-collar workers	1.1	4
White-collar workers	———	4
Civil servants	1.1	4
Farmers	———	———
Elementary teachers	———	———
Secondary and college teachers	6.6	14
Journalists	———	———
Doctors	1.1	4
Judges	18.7	6
Senior civil servants	60	30
Engineers[1]	9.9	12
Management	———	2
Merchants	———	———
Industrialists	———	6
Officers	3.3	16
Total	100 [N = 91]	100 [N = 50]

1. Public sector.

the best-represented corps are the prefects (28, or 38.4 percent), the overseas administrators (17, or 23.4 percent), and the diplomats (6, or 8.2 percent). The large number of overseas administrators results solely from the way these officials were reintegrated into the metropolitan administration. Of greater significance is the presence of so many prefects, initially justifiable as a reflection of their administrative experience, particularly on the ministerial staffs. It should not be forgotten, however, as Jeanne Siwek-Pouydesseau has observed, that "the prefectural corps is, owing to the very nature of its functions, the most politicized of the Grands Corps."[17] While the prefectural corps supposedly defends the general interest at the *départemental* level, it is nonetheless the principal agent of the central authorities, their most faithful servant. Merely because prefects are distinguished for displaying the virtue of obedience, however, it does not necessarily follow that the Conseil d'Etat is highly politicized: still, the habit of obedience does facilitate a certain interchange between the political powers and the bureaucracy. Just as the large number of prefectural corps members serving on ministerial staffs in the Fifth Republic implies that the corps is participating directly in the political administration of the system, so, too, does the presence of many corps members on the Conseil d'Etat as special appointees lead us to believe that the ties between this particular corps and the political authorities have become particularly close.[18] Accordingly, while it must still be stressed that no one from the private sector (industry, commerce, management) has secured (ordinary) special appointment to the Conseil, thus providing fresh proof of the degree to which the bureaucracy protects its autonomy by keeping out interlopers from the private business sector, we have nevertheless detected even at this stage signs of relatively close contact between the Conseil d'Etat and the powers-that-be in the world of politics.

Next, we shall look not at the professional backgrounds of the special appointees but at the posts they held just prior to being named to the Conseil. To begin with, table 5.4 confirms that few individuals from the private sector have gained access to the Conseil: among the extraordinary appointees, we find only one member of the CNPF and one member of the UIMM. Again looking at the extraordinary appointees, we see how few unionized workers are represented, those present being selected, moreover, on explicitly political grounds. For example, in 1964 those nominated included the man who had been the secretary-general of the Force Ouvrière until 1963, when he became a member of the board of the Banque de France, and the honorary president of the CFDT, who served as an administrator of the Crédit lyonnais from 1961 to 1967 and also as a member of the Conseil économique et social. In 1967 the president of the CFTC took a seat on the Conseil d'Etat. These exceptions notwithstanding, the main point to remember is that the group of extraordinary special appointees consisted chiefly of bureaucratic officials.

Looking next at the ordinary special appointees, we notice right away the large percentage of ministerial staff directors

TABLE 5.4 Last Post Held by Special Appointees to the Conseil d'Etat

Extraordinary Special Appointments	%	Conseillers	Ordinary Special Appointments %	Maîtres des requêtes	%
Faculty dean	6	College professor	5	Secondary and college teachers	3.2
College professor	12	Civil service post	13.3	Civil service post	22.4
General, admiral	10	Judge	16.6	Judges	9.6
Politician	2	Ministry staff director	38.3	Ministry staff director	3.2
Manager of public firm	14	Head of public firm	5	Ministerial staff	58
Business association representative	4	Ministerial staff	18.3	Politician	3.2
Union official	10	Miscellaneous	3.3		
Ministry staff director	26	Politician	—		
Civil service post	12				
Ministerial staff	4				

and staff members. The staff directors can be dealt with briefly: more than half the men who hold these positions do not feel they have reached the pinnacle of their careers.[19] It is a matter of tradition, for example, that directors in the Ministry of Justice are named after five years to serve as councillors on the Cour de cassation or the Conseil d'Etat. This is just one more sign of the tight control maintained by the administration.

The second point is worthy of lengthier commentary. The fact is that 18.3 percent of the conseillers and, even more noteworthy, 58 percent of the maîtres des requêtes served on ministerial staffs just prior to being named to these posts. Now, to serve in a staff position requires showing a modicum of support for the minister's policy, support which often increases during the period of staff tenure.[20] Even if the individuals in question have put in lengthy years in the administration before moving to their ministerial staff posts, we may assume that prior to their appointment to the Conseil d'Etat they gave certain assurance of political loyalty. Furthermore, it is worth noting that some individuals have managed to serve only briefly in the administration before gaining access to the Conseil d'Etat, using certain relatively highly politicized staffs as stepping-stones. Under the Fifth Republic, for example, six individuals who worked on the staffs of the president, the secretary-general of the government, and the prime minister were promoted to the Conseil d'Etat for explicitly political reasons. We may conclude, therefore, that while the Conseil d'Etat has remained almost completely closed to the private business sector, it is open to political influence from the government. As a result, the governmental machinery is probably more unified that it would otherwise be.[21]

The Cour des comptes

Scrutiny of the professional background of special appointees to the Cour des comptes reveals an even more clear-cut intention to restrict outside access. While most of the members of the Cour are admitted as *auditeurs* after graduation from the ENA, others are named, even today, as special appointees at the prerogative of the political authorities. For instance, the *procureurs généraux,* who stand at the top of the Cour des comptes hierarchy, are all named at the discretion of the government. As for the *conseillers maîtres,* one out of three is named by the government, the only requirements being that the individuals selected must be at least forty years of age and must have put in at least fifteen years of government service, and half of them must have worked in the Finances bureaucracy. As for the *conseillers référendaires,* they are no special appointments, but one post out of four is reserved for candidates from Finances. In all, slightly less than a third of the posts connected with the Cour des comptes are filled by special appointment.

Table 5.5 shows the professional backgrounds of 109 persons named to the corps by special appointment, as determined from information published in the *Annuaire de la Cour* from 1958 to 1974.

TABLE 5.5   Professional Background of Special Appointees to the Cour des Comptes

	N	%
Finance Ministry bureaucrat	52	85
Prefectoral corps	6	10
Diplomatic corps	1	1
Military	1	1
Bureaucrat in overseas territories	1	1
Elementary teacher	1	1
Engineer	1	1

We notice immediately that officials from Finances are overrepresented, the Cour serving explicitly as a means of promotion for members of the Finances bureaucracy. This more or less closed recruitment again helps to unify the governmental apparatus and adds to its functional autonomy. The fact that no one from the private sector gained access to the Cour has the same effect: even more than the Conseil d'Etat, the Cour des comptes recruits only within the bureaucracy; only civil servants manage to obtain appointments. The large number of prefectural corps members represented on the Cour should be noted, however, This affinity stands out even more clearly when we look at the last post held prior to special appointment to the Cour. Among appointees not coming from the Finances bureaucracy, we find the following distribution:

prefectural corps	66.6 percent
diplomatic corps	8.6 percent
civilian officials from Morocco	8.6 percent
public corporation directors	8.6 percent

In other words, we find evidence of the same phenomenon noted previously in connection with special appointments to the Conseil d'Etat, only in less pronounced form. In both cases (though in a considerably smaller proportion for the Cour des comptes), the prefectural corps, which has an undeniable political tinge, has succeeded in gaining access to these two Grands Corps.

Table 5.6 shows the last posts held by officials from Finances before their nomination to the Cour des comptes. Thus, in an appreciable proportion of the cases, the post held just prior to special appointment to the Cour was on a ministerial staff. As with the prefects, however, this proportion is noticeably smaller for the Cour than for the Conseil d'Etat. Still, it is a sign of some degree of politicization of special appointments to this Grand Corps. Furthermore, in addition to the four individuals in our sample who were appointed to the Cour after very brief stints in the administration, two more persons have been appointed on explicitly political grounds since the completion of our research.[22] Taking into account both members of the prefectural corps[23] and individuals who used the ministerial staffs as stepping-stones to the Cour, we find that the political authorities do exert some control over the Cour des comptes, though to a lesser degree than in the case of the Conseil d'Etat.

The Prefectural Corps

Since the diplomatic corps has its own peculiar mode of recruitment apparently based on different criteria, we felt it would be more interesting to take a quick look at nominations to the prefectural corps, which plays a crucial role in unifying the government and the bureaucracy, as we have already seen several times. Until 1964 prefects were appoint-

TABLE 5.6	Last Post Held by Finance Ministry Bureaucrats before Receiving Special Appointment to the Cour des Comptes	
	N	%
Staff head	10	11.1
Public prosecutor	4	4.5
Head of office or department	19	21.3
Tax collector	1	1.1
Civil administrator	35	39.3
Editor	2	2.2
Chief inspector for registration	3	3.4
Ministerial staff subsequent to long career in the bureaucracy	12	12.1
Ministerial staff only	4	4.5

ed at the sole discretion of the government; the decree of July 29, 1964, however, which was designed to stabilize the corps and upgrade the professional qualifications of its personnel,[24] specifies that at least four-fifths of new prefects must come from the corps of subprefects and civil administrators. This reform has increased the tendency of the senior civil service to recruit from within its own ranks and has thereby heightened its distinctive functional character. For the purposes of our analysis, then, we shall regard a nomination as a special appointment when the individual promoted is neither a subprefect nor a civil administrator.

Once again, senior civil servants are virtually alone in entering the prefectural corps by special appointment to the highest-level posts. Between July 1, 1958, and December 31, 1975, only fourteen persons were nominated in this manner: two members of the Conseil d'Etat, one member of the Inspection des Finances, two of the Cour des comptes, three senior police officials, two governors of overseas territories, and, finally, two members of the technical corps. Only two persons were not drawn from the ranks of the civil service, and they held political posts (Pierre Lefranc, Olivier Guichard): just prior to their nominations, moreover, they served on General de Gaulle's staff.

The political aspect of these two appointments takes on its full significance when we observe that out of the twelve other appointees, only four (including the three police officials) did not serve on ministerial staffs: indeed, in almost all cases the staffs involved were those of the prime minister or the minister of the interior, which are particularly highly politicized. It would seem, then, that the special appointees had either served on ministerial staffs which had a clear-cut political coloration or had held posts which in almost all cases required some political commitment.

Finally, if we look briefly at special appointments to the subprefectural ranks, we find that between 1959 and 1961 these were used largely for the purpose of reassigning large numbers of senior officials from overseas territories; between 1966 and 1975 the corps accepted some police officials and regular army officers. Once again, the bureaucracy preserved its distinctive character by closing access to individuals from the private sector. Frequently, however, it did accept as special appointees persons who in one way or another had shown their political allegiance, at the risk "of compromising, as an incumbent prefect observed, the efficiency of the provincial administration."[25]

The fact that special appointments to the Grands Corps draw so heavily on the senior ranks of the civil service leads one to believe that in the future the Corps will be staffed increasingly by ENA graduates, those who entered the less exalted areas of the bureaucracy upon graduation later rejoining those of their former classmates lucky enough to go directly into the Grands Corps after completion of their schooling. This process of internal recruitment, which virtually closes access to the private sector and particularly to private business, seems likely to encourage the formation of an autonomous and homogeneous elite of senior officials, a development which will inevitably increase the distance between the bureaucracy and civil society even further. However, while the Grands Corps are protected against intrusion by businessmen, they are nevertheless subject to political influence,[26] which affects their recruitment to some extent; furthermore, they have lately been taking a direct hand in government, sending many members to work on ministerial staffs and increasingly to sit within the government itself. Thus the mutual interchange between the upper reaches of the bureaucracy and the government has been steadily on the rise under the Fifth Republic: concretely, this interchange has taken the form of increased participation of senior bureaucrats in the government, with the government in turn interfering in the recruitment of civil service personnel as well as in the day-to-day operations of the administrative bureaucracy. The increasing solidarity between bureaucracy and government under the Fifth Republic accounts for the state's claim that it is acting independently in such a way as to organize as it thinks best the social system as a whole, and in particular the future course of business activities.

6 Government Control over Economic Life

The increasing unity of the government and the bureaucracy has been reflected in the ever tighter control exerted by the state over the economic life of the nation, and has gone hand in hand with ever greater exclusion of parliament from major economic decision-making. Members of parliament have increasingly concerned themselves with the administration of local affairs and have given up any pretense of exerting genuine control over the specific actions of the high administration, particularly in the area of economic policy. In the same vein, parliament has been less and less involved in drawing up each new economic plan.[1]

The split between parliament and the government has also led to a shift in the focus of action by pressure groups, which have adjusted to the decline in the importance of parliament by concentrating their activities on the ministers and senior bureaucrats who hold the real trumps in determining economic policy. Thus Henry Ehrmann has shown how the pressure groups have been "deserting" the corridors of the Palais Bourbon* since 1958 and "now do their work almost exclusively in the offices of the bureaucracy."[2] Under the Fifth Republic, the pressure groups, particularly those representing big business, have directly lobbied the senior bureaucrats who are in close contact with the ministries and other centers of power in the executive branch.[3]

From Gaullist Planning to Giscardian Liberalism

The lobbyists do not, however, determine in any mechanical way how the government and the bureaucracy will act; the high administration has its own distinctive functions, is a cohesive unit, and acts in accordance with a vision of the

*Where parliament meets.—Trans.

world derived from its own notions of efficiency, so that the government is able to put up quite a solid front against social pressures, including pressure from businessmen. In this regard, the creation of the ENA —now the training ground for a considerable proportion of the Grands Corps members who subsequently move on to serve on ministerial staffs and in some cases to become ministers themselves—has been a crucial factor.

Prior to the Second World War, most senior civil servants were trained as lawyers and were somewhat loath to study economics. After 1945, however, at the behest of General de Gaulle and Michel Debré, the ENA began turning out students well versed in applied economics[4] and imbued with a deep feeling for the state and public service, which they saw as connected with promotion of the general interest. Strangers to the political compromises they looked upon as the stock-in-trade of the traditional politician, these senior civil servants claimed to incarnate Spirit itself and to act solely in the name of rationality. A functional bureaucracy came into being whose self-image matched the ideal-type described by Max Weber, a bureaucracy that claimed all the virtues Hegel attributed to the Prussian bureaucracy. Totally identified with their official mission, the ENA graduates see themselves as "embodiments of their roles," "men without qualities" other than those that attest to their skills and legitimize their power: "their notion of the state and their mystique of expansion mingle in their minds, and the result is a vision in which the administration plays the preponderant role,"[5] acting in the name of the general interest and free, we are told, of any partisan or ideological taint. With a view of the world predicated on planning and interventionism under the aegis of rationality, these highly trained officials have worked to create a state capable of arbitrating conflicts by reducing social tensions, integrating society from above. In their view, the rationality that guides their action guarantees neutrality: the more state intervention is guided solely by scientific knowledge and expertise, they argue, the more legitimate that action will be.

From its inception, then, the purpose of the ENA has been, as General de Gaulle put it, to enable the state to act "above the parties." With the birth of the Fifth Republic the role of the ENA was to increase dramatically, the man behind its founding in 1945, Michel Debré, becoming prime minister and proclaiming at once that he favored an interventionist policy supposedly tailored to promote the general interest. Incidentally, it should be noted that in this respect Gaullism harks back to policies first conceived by Louis XIV, who used his *intendants* to establish centralized control over French society, as well as to policies of Napoleon III, who used the prefects to "guide"[6] society and oversee the organization of the economy. Beyond the ideological character of the claims made in behalf of such policies, we find that the model of the state implicit in them has other consequences, signs of which turn up when we look, for example, at the activist economic policies adopted in the early years of the Fifth Republic.

Under plans drawn up at the behest of General de Gaulle and Michel Debré, the state's senior bureaucrats sought to accelerate France's industrial development during this period by modernizing the productive apparatus. To this end, these officials, most of whom were ENA graduates, were obliged to combat the very deep-seated Malthusianism prevalent among French businessmen and often had to force industrialists to go along with economic measures of which they scarcely approved. These were the early days of the new "Colbertism," the goal of which was to make the state independent. Gaullism's opposition to certain business conservatives made itself felt from the very first days of the Fifth Republic: the minister of finance, Antoine Pinay, quickly came into conflict with technocrats who were promoting state capitalism by setting up, among other things, a company to market gasoline nationwide.

More generally, the industrial expansion favored by the top bureaucrats, who had the support of General de Gaulle, encountered the hostility of protectionist businessmen, symbolized in the person of Antoine Pinay: indeed, members of the PME* often had interests contrary to those of large firms in leading sectors of the economy, which could more easily adapt to the objectives laid down by the Plan. The political authorities and their senior bureaucratic officials therefore

---

*The trade association representing small- and medium-sized businesses.—Trans.

faced a dilemma, which has continued to plague the Fifth Republic to this day: they had to hold on to the political support of the middle classes and small businessmen in order to preserve a majority in parliament, while at the same time implementing an interventionist economic strategy aimed at large-scale industrialization and concentration, which could only work against the interests of small businesses and hasten their demise. It becomes easy to understand, then, how certain Communist leaders could have seen in Gaullism the emergence of a new form of capitalism. The reader will recall (see chapter 1) that in 1960-61, Communist leaders saw Gaullism as a nationalist form of capitalism pitted against the PME in league with international capitalism, which also opposed the expansion of any independent form of capitalism though for reasons different from those of the PME. The ambition to provide the state with an economic base of its own grew out of the Gaullist desire to create a state capable of acting independently through its functionally specialized bureaucracy. This aspect of Gaullism, perhaps chiefly a reflection of one strand of Gaullist ideology, quickly receded as the regime evolved and was ultimately supplanted by the "Pompidou system," about which we shall have more to say later on: still, this drive for independence had been behind the interventionist thrust in Gaullist planning, which caused deep splits within French capitalism.

Indeed, French industry has long been characterized by a dualist structure in which two kinds of production have coexisted: on the one hand, large-scale, modernized, highly concentrated firms, manufacturing standardized products in large quantities and seeking constantly to diversify their output, and, on the other hand, small- and medium-sized firms, set up to produce one unit at a time and run in much more traditional ways than the large, modern firms. Moreover, the present situation only continues the structure of nineteenth-century capitalism. As Guy Palmade has pointed out, the variety of organizational types in industry has given rise to a diverse range of businessmen and trade associations.[7]

In the first half of the nineteenth century the institutional basis of the economy lay with the individual and the family: businessmen in this period were cautious, paternalistic, and had an old-fashioned outlook. The second half of the nineteenth century saw some concentration of production and an increase in profits that benefited the leading industrial families and impelled them to arrange strategic marriages aimed at further consolidation of their economic power. The first half of the twentieth century was to be the era of big business and concentration in the full sense of the word; some observers, though, have held that the concentration process was not carried far enough, because it never really eliminated the fundamentally dualistic structure of the economy.[8] According to Maurice Lévy-Leboyer, French businessmen were not deliberately Malthusian and did not intentionally impede the modernization process. However that may be, differences in the size and interests of various production units persist today and explain the bitter conflicts that have arisen among different business groups.

Differences between firms are particularly apparent in the area of management personnel. Unlike members of the PME, large-scale concentrated firms have been turning more and more to technically trained graduates of the Grandes Ecoles, who are often more interested in expanding the firm than in adding to its profits. This observation, which Galbraith has made of contemporary capitalism in general, is applicable to large French firms, many of which have grown to quite considerable proportions under the Fifth Republic. Regardless of whether or not this development poses a threat to private ownership of the means of production, it does account for the growing complicity between senior bureaucrats and managers of highly concentrated business firms. The shared outlook and methods of these two groups did not take on their full significance until the shift to neo-liberal policies in 1962-65. These factors became even more important with the advent of Giscardism in 1974.

Before we examine these neo-liberal policies, the contradictions between the different sectors of the economy that developed in the early days of Gaullism deserve further comment. 1958 marks the inception of the Third Plan, which deliberately aimed to promote rapid growth. As General de Gaulle saw it, "the plan takes in the whole, sets the goals, and establishes priorities of urgency and importance."[9] Similarly, according to Michel Debré, under the Plan "the higher interest of the nation must take precedence over the particular interests of firms or groups of firms."[10] In this regard, both Michel Debré and Jean-Marcel Jeanneney sought to increase state intervention in the economy in order to facilitate industrial transformation, modernization, and concentration and thereby encourage production for export. With the aid of the Plan, together with regional development plans, the state showed itself more capable than businessmen themselves of stimulating economic innovation.[11]

This activist policy was continued under the Fourth Plan, which remained France's "great affair," in the words of General de Gaulle. The state even reserved the right to set up new businesses should the private sector fail to act. The senior civil service, the extent of whose distinctive functional role we have already indicated, thus played a fundamental part in the regulation of the economy: far from being a mere instrument of capitalism, the senior civil service, which had also taken over the executive, worked toward an economic policy that was in the long-term interest of businessmen but nevertheless ran up against their hostility for the time being. Such top officials as François Bloch-Lainé, Pierre Massé, and Claude Gruson aimed at all costs to hasten modernization of the economy, if need be at the expense of conservative elements in the society. The concentration of power in government and bureaucracy thus facilitated concentration in the economy, leaving parliament to serve as a sounding board for the complaints of social groups injured by modernization and allowing the traditional politicians to work out the compromises necessary to preserve the democratically elected majority.

The government and bureaucracy have enjoyed rather considerable freedom of action despite this contradiction, which has persisted throughout the Fifth Republic despite various changes in economic policy. Thus the replacement of Michel Debré by Georges Pompidou in 1962 and the appointment of Valéry Giscard d'Estaing as minister of finance were early signs of a decreased emphasis on planning and a shift toward a policy of more liberal inspiration, a trend that was destined to continue; the liberal policy also encouraged concentration, but now in a manner determined by the laws of the marketplace and free competition, which once again would place small- and medium-sized firms in a difficult position. No longer was the Plan an end in itself, but only a means.

This shift became more pronounced in 1965, when a "neo-liberal" policy was adopted, entailing radical changes in the role accorded the Plan.[12] Convinced by now of the need for genuine competition, which alone could bring about modernization of large firms and increase export sales, businessmen began to assert more clearly their desire to control the development of the capitalist economy themselves: in consequence, the CNPF declared that it wished to "restrict the steady encroachment of the state."[13] From 1965 on, the pace of mergers picked up: first Pechiney-Saint-Gobain and Ugine-Kuhlmann, and later Boussois-Souchon-Neuvesel, as well as de Wendel joining Sidelor and the CGE joining Alsthom; Citroën took over Panhard before being swallowed up itself by Peugeot; and, finally, in the petroleum industry, ERAP was set up in 1965.

With the Fifth Plan, and even more with the Sixth, the state gave up its role as manager of the economy and limited its future role to one of promoting concentration, fostering competition, and encouraging export trade.[14] No longer did the Plan seem "a burning imperative": now it was used chiefly as a means of assisting large firms. As Lucien Nizard has observed, the planners "did not build French neo-capitalism from the ground up, they served as a catalyst, accelerating the changeover by creating the proper conditions for it to occur."[15] To that end, the bureaucracy invited representatives of large firms to work with the committees responsible for elaborating industrial policy: in 1965, for example, the Economic Development Committee created by Georges Pompidou included fourteen members: six inspecteurs des Finances, one union official, and several representatives of big business and banking interests. Similarly, in preparing his report in favor of free competition, Simon Nora surrounded himself with top bureaucrats and big business representatives, who struck an accord that called for "a strong dose of liberalism and healthy profits." As Gilles Martinet has observed, between 1965 and 1968 "the technocrats openly played the part of capitalism's 'organic' intellectuals."[16]

To carry out this policy, the minister of industry in 1967 created a Council on Industrial Progress made up of six senior bureaucrats and eight representatives of large firms, including Ambroise Roux, president of the CGE. It was quite logical for Georges Pompidou, even though he was by then no longer prime minister, to declare that "it is in the best interest of the country that businesses earn more profits."[17] From this time on, the activist policy sponsored by Michel Debré, which had claimed not to favor large enterprises, was apparently doomed. General de Gaulle's departure from office after the failure of the referendum on the regions of April 27, 1969, and Valéry Giscard d'Estaing's call for a "no" vote mark the end of Gaullism's ambiguities. Big business aimed to do away once and for all with activist Gaullist planning and instead to carry out its own economic policy: the state was ready to forgo its claim to independence, return to its former place in relation to civil society, and mend its traditional alliances with business and industry, whose policies it would no longer try to control.

Lionel Stoleru, who in 1969 became technical adviser in charge of industrial affairs on the staff of Valéry Giscard d'Estaing, then finance minister, and who would later serve as a minister in the Chirac government under Giscard's presidency, stated unequivocally in his book *L'Impératif industriel* that the quest for profits was a legitimate activity on the part of businesses which had no choice but to concentrate. He maintained that "to oppose this trend, on the pretext that the trusts thereby created will oppress the workers and exploit consumers by abusing their power, is to work against the laws of efficiency."[18] In the same vein, the Sixth Plan study committee set up by the Commissariat général du Plan and made up of senior civil servants such as Paul Delouvrier and Pierre Guillaumat, representatives of big business such as R. Martin (president of Pont-à-Mousson), and academics such as Raymond Aron and Michel Crozier, contended that "the basic themes of French economic modernization (industrialization, efficiency, competition) are the work of only a small segment of the population, namely, big businessmen and senior bureaucrats." On the other hand, "certain socioprofessional groups, who fail to see how they would profit by the proposed changes, have met these plans with passive resistance, sometimes tinged with anxiety."[19] The alliance between big business and government was forged on the basis of a common acceptance of the principle of free competition as a spur to industrial concentration. Henceforth the state and big business would share similar interests: the Gaullist desire for an independent state had evidently gone by the boards.

From this point on, government and big business were destined to grow closer and closer very rapidly, putting an end to the Gaullist version of Colbertism that had gone before. Jacques Chirac, as prime minister in a new government that included Lionel Stoleru and other ENA graduates, faithfully represented the state's new economic strategy. In introducing the Seventh Plan on July 1, 1976, he asserted that "the efficiency and competitiveness of French industry require above all that the state leave managers free to run their businesses as they see fit and to bear full responsibility for the choices they make. To date, planning has too often meant centralization, concentration, standardization, and regimentation."[20] The officials in charge of the bureaucracy rallied in support of economic liberalism and rejected state interventionism, which Michel Debré had at one time expected to promote the general interest rather than business interests. German and Japanese growth and fascination with the efficiency of large American companies were responsible for the demise of French-style planning.

Paradoxically, however, Jacques Chirac concluded his speech by saying that "the Seventh Plan inaugurates a turnabout, making development of small- and medium-sized firms a national priority."[21] In truth, economic liberalism spells doom for the PME and small craft shops and promises to aid the highly concentrated large-scale firms that are alone capable of coping with the competition. Thus we see fresh signs of a basic contradiction still in evidence today, between the state's unstinting support for big business firms and the damage done by their rapid growth to socioprofessional groups such as those represented by the PME, whose support on election day remains crucial to perpetuating the power of the majority.

The Royer Law, or the Contradictions in the State's Economic Policy

To understand the contradiction just alluded to, we may look at the circumstances surrounding the passage of the Royer Law on December 27, 1973. This issue brought to the surface serious conflicts within the majority between those in favor of modernizing retail distribution in France and those who, influenced by the four million or so small-merchant votes, were ready to defend an outmoded market structure in order to hold on to their seats in the Assembly.

Under the Fourth Republic, small merchants with political problems turned mainly to members of parliament, who counted on their support for reelection, while the capitalist retailers represented by the CNPF preferred to take their case directly to the senior officials concerned.[22] During this same period the Poujadist movement gave vent to the discontents of small merchants, who resented the Parisian technocrats they felt to be closely allied with big business. As Stanley Hoffmann has shown, the Poujadist movement was "an almost desperate outburst against one form of social change," change that saw the importance of the small-merchant class decline rapidly.[23] Food retailers, particularly small grocers, were particularly hard hit by the rise of large supermarkets. As Christian Baudelot, Roger Establet, and Jacques Malemort have observed, "the thrust of capitalism into the sphere of commerce manifested itself by an expansion of wage labor and a steady decline in the number of independent shopkeepers."[24]

Faced with contradictory demands, the government's economic policy at first tried deliberately to hasten the decline of small business in the name of economic efficiency. In 1959, fourteen experts joined in a group known as the Armand-Rueff Committee for the purpose of identifying the obstacles to expansion of integrated commerce. These experts proposed the abolition of all laws regulating the opening of larger stores, the elimination of higher licensing fees for corporations operating more than one sales outlet, gradual elimination of the contractual tax system that favored small merchants, and so forth. In 1951, the Fontanet memorandum prohibited discriminatory sales and pricing policies; a whole range of measures were subsequently enacted against small merchants:

rebates on stocks, elimination of double licensing, broadening of the value-added tax, and so on. In addition, the state encouraged concentration of capital in the commercial sector through its nationalized banks, such as the Crédit lyonnais and Société générale, which participated in the Union immobilière des supermarchés et des centres commerciaux.*

In 1969, however, the authorities looked on with trepidation as a new movement spread among small merchants and vehemently made its views known: the CID UNATI, led by Gérard Nicoud. Indeed, this movement threatened to undermine the majority in the coming elections. Accordingly, Georges Pompidou took measures to calm the situation and in his speeches developed an apology for small business. Named to fill the newly created post of secretary of state for commerce was Jean Royer, who was destined to become the ardent champion of small merchants in their fight against large-scale capitalism in the retail sector. The government's contradictory economic policy culminated in the Royer Law of December 27, 1973.

Government economic policy had increased competition, hastened the closure of many small shops, and encouraged the creation of large retail stores, which were able to offer reduced prices and attract increasing numbers of customers away from small merchants owing to the various advantages of large-scale operations and rapid turnover. Thus the number of independent small merchants was reduced by the advent of supermarkets and discount stores, which soon dotted the areas of new urban growth. The first large discount store was opened at Sainte-Geneviève-des-Bois in 1963; by the beginning of 1973, there were 209 discount stores and 2,337 supermarkets in France, which by themselves accounted for 22 percent of food sales. Moreover, the supermarket sector was itself highly concentrated, with 51 chains owning 209 supermarkets, which 5 chains owned 105 of the discount stores: Carrefour, Escale, Rond Point, Mammouth, Radar; 10 chains owned 177 of the discount stores, or 69 percent of the total.[25]

In line with the liberal economic policy followed by then finance minister Valéry Giscard d'Estaing, this very rapid

---

*An investment group that provided financing for supermarkets and shopping malls.—Trans.

growth of large retail stores cut into the business of the traditional small merchants, who organized to fight the trend. Gérard Nicoud's CID UNATI grew rapidly to substantial proportions throughout France thanks to the help of a large number of well-organized volunteer activists. Not only did this movement mount violent demonstrations, but small merchants made their electoral power felt by helping to defeat the 1969 referendum and to oust Maurice Couve de Murville from office in the Yvelines by-election. It was then that the government, in order to hold on to the votes necessary to maintain its parliamentary majority, agreed to halt modernization of the retail sector in response to the fiscal and social demands put forward by the small merchants. To that end, Jean Royer, minister of commerce and spokesmen within the councils of government for a provincial France firmly wedded to the past, filed a bill, article 21 of which gave small merchants the right to decide whether or not large retail stores or supermarkets could be opened in their area. This was accomplished by empowering the *départemental* commissions on urban planning, in which small merchants played a key role (thanks to article 22 of this same bill), to make such decisions.

In the long parliamentary debate that ensued, it is worth noting that it was Valéry Giscard d'Estaing who adopted a conciliatory attitude, while Michel Debré and Maurice Couve de Murville, who assumed the mantle of Gaullism, were firm in their outspoken hostility to the state's relinquishing any of its prerogatives in favor of a particular social group. Indeed, the Gaullist vision of the state inevitably implies a blunt and uncompromising rejection of the corporatism of special-interest groups. Now, however, under the terms of the Royer Law, the prefects were stripped of part of their power, since decisions formerly made by them alone in the name of the state were henceforth subject to the consent of commissions in which small merchants sat as judges as well as parties in the case.

By contrast, in Jean Royer's view, "the merchants are France," the France of the provinces as opposed to the France of concentrated capitalism. The senior bureaucrats, who rejected this backward vision of France, were nevertheless ready to overlook this challenge to their professed liberalism in economic matters, for they were aware of the strength of the small merchants at the polls. However, one faction of the majority—somewhat surprisingly, among the Independent Republicans—remained deaf to the demands of the small merchants and more alive to those of the retail chains. Out of these differences there arose a debate in parliament and a series of highly instructive votes.

An amendment proposed by Jean Poperen was aimed at changing the makeup of the *départemental* commissions in order to reduce the representation of the small merchants. This amendment was supported by a fairly substantial segment of the majority, even though it went against the thrust of the bill submitted by the government. Furthermore, certain deputies in the majority refused to vote for the clause empowering these commissions to make decisions. Under rather unusual circumstances, the government proposed a new amendment, restoring the power of the small merchants. This time almost all the deputies of the majority voted for the amendment, including those who had voted against the initial language of the bill.

We have looked more closely at the deputies who first voted against granting extensive powers to the commissions and then, one week later, voted for the amendment that restored the original content of the Royer Bill, gave merchants significant representation on the commissions and thus in effect gave them the power to accept or reject new construction of large retail stores. Forty-six deputies were involved, thirty-seven of them members of the majority who at first opposed the government and then voted with Jean Royer. Some of them, such as Pierre de Benouville and Gabriel Daspereit were connected with chain stores as officials or shareholders; on the other hand, Daniel Goulet, a member of the board of Goulet-Turpin, supported the government's bill from the first, even though it was unfavorable to large stores.[26]

Given these differences in behavior, it is more interesting to look at what types of *départements* were represented by deputies who changed their votes. It turns out that they came mainly from regions where large stores were most widespread, namely, the Paris area, the regions between the Rhône and the Alps, in Provence, and along the Côte d'Azur. These are also the areas in which the more traditional forms of retail commerce had also made progress, thus increasing the proportion of small merchants. We may conclude, then, that the deputies who changed their votes were in many cases those who, apart from standing up for their Gaullist or Jacobin convictions, were caught between pressures of two opposite kinds: they had to appease both the small merchants on whom they were largely dependent for reelection and the chain-store owners who had the means to exert strong pressure. By contrast, in the Nord, for example, where chain stores were making rapid headway while small business remained stagnant, the deputies did not behave in this contradictory way.

The violent demonstrations of the CID UNATI rapidly overcame the hesitations of deputies who at first had been favorably disposed to the chain stores. Still, it should be noted that even though the Independent Republicans did rally in support of the government bill sponsored by Jean Royer, they were astute enough to express their reservations at every turn. Valéry Giscard d'Estaing, for example, worked to limit the tax concessions won by the small merchants, and his opposition to the Royer bill, which he had cosponsored, was apparent to all. On August 5, for example, he declared that "the question is one of setting limits to competition without being hostile to competition in itself. Otherwise, we would be favoring higher prices and hindering the modernization of retail trade, which is far from complete."[27] Similarly, Roger Chinaud, later secretary-general of the Independent Republicans, opposed the Royer bill, as did M. Boisdé, then vice-president of the party.

Though all these individuals in the end rallied in support of the government's bill, it is worthy of note that alongside such confirmed Gaullists and Jacobins as Michel Debré and Maurice Couve de Murville it was mainly the champions of the economic liberalism that was guiding the state's overall economic policy who, for reasons of their own, displayed hostility to a law that hindered the spread of chain stores and weakened the grip of large-scale capital on the economy. Furthermore, it should be noted that Pierre Abelin, Michel Durafour, Jean Lecanuet, Gabriel Peronnet, and Jean-Jacques Servan-

Schreiber, at this date still members of the opposition, were among those who abstained from voting on the government amendment in favor of the small merchants. All of them would later become ministers in the Chirac government under Giscard's presidency. The alliance between Giscardism and the deputies of the center-right, enamored of modernization and favorably disposed toward the "Anglo-Saxon" model of economic development, had already taken concrete form in this more or less explicit common rejection of outmoded economic forms, which the Royer Law allowed to linger on. The law proved quite effective, moreover, since in 1975 the *départemental* urban planning commissions had majorities opposed to the further spread of chain stores: these majorities were composed of representatives of small merchants joined in many cases by other small businessmen who sat on the commissions in their capacity as local officeholders. Among them were also skilled craftsmen and hotelkeepers, who in certain localities assisted the small merchants in effectively halting the spread of chain stores.[28]

The Royer Law makes quite clear how far those in power, who favored modern, highly concentrated capitalism, have been obliged to remain attentive to the demands of social groups that are basically hostile to large-scale capitalism but nevertheless express the deep-seated wishes of a substantial portion of the populace and carry great weight at the ballot box. As noted earlier, this is one reason why these groups are particularly influential with parliament: we have seen, for example, how deputies beaten in elections continue to enjoy considerable prestige locally and succeed in obtaining leadership positions with local firms and agencies. By contrast, those at the top of government and the bureaucracy are in closer contact with big business, and when they leave office often take seats on the boards of directors of national firms. Often responding to contradictory requirements, the economic policy of the Fifth Republic has not hindered the establishment of ever closer relations between government leaders and big businessmen.

The Commissions d'Industrialisation

The industrialization commissions (commissions d'industrialisation du Plan) seem to play a key role in the elaboration of economic policy, whether that policy is in one degree or another based on activism and planning or limited to the encouragement of free competition as desired by those in favor of going back to economic liberalism. These commissions make the major decisions affecting modernization of the economy and concentration of the productive apparatus in the face of international competition. Their deliberations, so they claim, are based on economic rationality.

As far as possible insulated from the electoral concerns so apparent in the Royer Law, these commissions pay scant attention to protecting the interests of small merchants and almost always display vigorous hostility to outmoded ways of doing business. Hence the makeup of these commissions from the time of the Fourth Plan to that of the present Seventh Plan should prove interesting to study.[29]

If we look at the "positional space" of commission members under the Fourth and Fifth plans, that is, the variety of positions held by each actor in the different areas of the social system (political, economic, administrative, and cultural),[30] we find that the space occupied by the eighty-nine members of these commissions is rather limited; in other words, many of them held positions in only one area of the social system. Among these the economic area seems to be predominant, for only six cannot be connected in some way with it: these six are all senior civil servants. All the others fall into the economic sphere: sixty-four industrialists, five top managers from the private sector, and fourteen members of unions representing workers and supervisors. The different areas of the social system are highly compartmentalized, few of the bureaucrats having political or business qualifications, while those from the business world are only rarely involved in the government or bureaucracy. Furthermore, it should be noted that 56 percent of the commission members are the offspring of industrialists or bankers, and 31 percent of top management or engineers. Thus the economic policy of the state was elaborated in the commissions by industrialists who did not themselves take part in government activities as such. There was close contact between government and business, but the personnel on either side remained distinct.

By contrast, the membership of the industrialization commissions under the Sixth Plan, which favored economic liberalization and halted the planning that Gaullist policy had promoted, was fundamentally different from that of earlier commissions. Out of ninety-two individuals (including, in addition to the industrialization commission, the Ortoli-Montjoie commission, which met during approximately the same period), only three were not drawn from the economic sector. The commission members included thirty-seven industrialists and heads of commercial firms, twenty-three bank and insurance company directors, eight directors of public-sector firms, and fifteen top managers from the banking sector as well as five from the public sector. Although the economic area was still overwhelmingly predominant, the various sectors were no longer distinct and autonomous. Fifty of the ninety-two individuals had at one time or another worked in the administration: forty for some department of the central government, twenty-four with the Inspection des Finances, three each with the Conseil d'Etat and Cour des comptes, ten with the corps of engineers. The interpenetration of business and the governmental bureaucracy is thus quite evident and significant. Then, too, many of these individuals had played important political roles, which formerly was almost never the case. In earlier commissions only one person had served on a ministerial staff; by contrast, twenty-seven members of the Sixth Plan's industrialization commission and the Ortoli-Montjoie group had worked on such staffs, sixteen of them coming from the Inspection des Finances and fourteen having served on the staff of the finance minister. Notice, finally, that of the fifty-three individuals who held important administrative posts, thirty-nine later became directors of large private-sector firms. In other words, the ties between the administrative, political, and economic sectors were becoming closer and closer during this period. The point to remember is that the governmental apparatus, while preserving its functional autonomy, came to take an increasingly prominent role in the management of the private sector: within the industrialization commissions, the negotiations were often carried on between senior bureaucrats who had remained in government and their former colleagues who had gone into the private sector.

This commission, largely responsible for deciding what the economic policy of France would be, was thus a place where top bureaucrats and businessmen mingled, the latter often represented by former bureaucrats anointed by the powers-that-be during stints on ministerial staffs prior to their transfer to the private sector. Under the Fifth Republic, then, the mobility of senior civil servants insured that leadership groups within the society would be of homogeneous composition and contributed to making the influence of the governmental apparatus crucial in determining what went on in civil society and particularly in the world of business, which seemed increasingly incapable of controlling its own activities. This unity, to which we shall return below, also reveals how far from the major centers of decision-making parliament had become; while in the commissions top bureaucrats dealt with former colleagues now representing big business after staff service in the ministries, in parliament the deputies were bogged down in lengthy debate over the Royer Law and were impelled by the realities of the ballot box to accord tremendous power to the small merchant class. The separation of powers, never so great as now, should not be allowed to conceal the new unity that reigns at the top of the government, with the bureaucracy delegating some of its members to serve big business in the private sector while at the same time maintaining absolute control over the public sector.

The new contacts that we see between business and government in the commission associated with the Sixth Plan were perpetuated under the Seventh Plan, whose commission was named in January 1975 and is still in existence as of this writing (1976). The first such commission to be appointed under Giscard's presidency, the Commission on Growth, Employment, and Investment, with thirty-one members, supplanted the industrialization commissions of the earlier Plans. Only seven of its members were not industrialists; that business was all-powerful did not mean that the administration was squeezed out, for 63 percent of the commission membership consisted of men who had held bureaucratic posts.[31] Almost all of these individuals had worked for departments of the central government, half of them came from the Inspection des Finances, there being far fewer representatives (only one, in fact) of the corps of engineers than on earlier commissions. The number of individuals who had played some political role, already considerable on the commission for the Sixth Plan, was now even higher, up from 50 percent to 60 percent. Fifty percent of these had served on ministerial staffs (or 30 percent of the full membership of the commission, compared with 25 percent for the preceding one). All members who had served on ministerial staffs had come from the senior civil service, and two-thirds of them had worked for the minister of finance. Similarly, half of those who had worked in the central bureaucracy had headed major departments within the finance ministry while Giscard was minister.

We also witness a gradual change in the social background of commission members: fewer and fewer come from industrial families, while an ever-increasing number are civil servants, reflecting the invasion of industry by the bureaucrats, who become its spokesmen. Under the Fourth Plan, 56 percent of commission members were offspring of industrialists, compared with only 38 percent under the Sixth Plan and 27 percent under the Seventh. Conversely, the number of offspring of senior civil servants increased steadily from one commission to the next.

The changes in these commissions, which play an important role in determining the state's economic policy, are indicative of an increasing interpenetration of bureaucracy and business, the result, it would seem, not so much of diffusion of personnel in both directions as of an increasingly tight control of business by senior functionaries, often offspring of former officials engaged in negotiations with former colleagues gone over to private industry. Big business is apparently incapable of representing itself, since the task of negotiating with the government in the industrial commissions is assigned to former government officials who have moved into the private sector. The final point to be gleaned from investigating the makeup of the industrial commissions is that "pantouflage" is very common: the bureaucracy, not content to manage the economy through the machinery of government, in particular the Plan, has moved to control big business from within by taking over key jobs in the private sector.

"Pantouflage," or the Bureaucratic Exodus

The interpenetration of bureaucracy and big business has been further increased by pantouflage, with senior functionaries reaping all the benefits as they take over important jobs in the private sector; industrialists, on the other hand, almost never succeed in cracking the bureaucracy, which has been able to preserve its distinctive functional character.[32] Because of the rapid concentration of big business, large firms have been attracting top bureaucrats eager to put their economic skills to work in management capacities. When the Plan was still a "burning necessity," bureaucrats used their skills to encourage concentration from without, hastening modernization of the productive apparatus by application of government power. Once this was accomplished, these same bureaucrats, few of whom came from industrial families, went into the manufacturing sector where the economic ideas to which they subscribed were being applied, later returning to some cases to the service of the state.

As Pierre Bourdieu, Luc Boltanski, and Monique de Saint-Martin have observed, "the transformation of the structures of the economy has gone hand in hand with a transformation of the structures of the firm, which in turn has necessitated a change in the qualifications of management personnel and in the nature of management itself, hence in the structure of authority within the firm."[33] The new industrial managers now tend to be graduates in law or political science if not of the ENA, with the number of graduates of scientific schools and the Ecole Polytechnique falling off somewhat by comparison;[34] the academic training of the new managers gives them a vision of the world close to that of top bureaucrats in the government.

Apart from this common cultural background, stress must also be laid on the growing importance of "pantouflage," the transfer of government bureaucrats into private business: for example, 12 percent of the heads of the top one hundred French companies have worked for the Inspection des Finances or the Cour des comptes, and 17 percent of these served on ministerial staffs before taking jobs in big business (see table 6.1).[35] Moreover, 43 percent of the heads of the top one hundred French companies have worked in the administration in one capacity or another, and 45 percent, often the same individuals, have had political experience.

Since these big businessmen in many instances also hold important posts in trade associations and, thanks to their

TABLE 6.1   Positions of Influence of Heads of Large Businesses, 1972

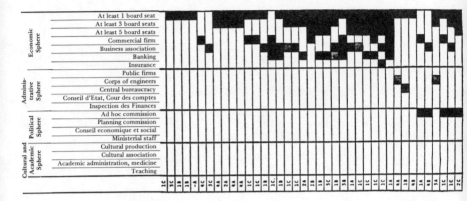

This table should read as follows: Each column corresponds to the head of one of the 100 largest French firms in 1972; each row corresponds to a specific type of position (e.g., a teaching post). The rows are grouped into four different spheres (e.g., academic and cultural sphere, economic sphere). A black square indicates that the individual in question presently occupies the corresponding post, a gray square indicates that he has occupied such a post in the past.

For the sake of clarity, it has been necessary to establish a nomenclature of positions and to group similar and related types of positions together: hence a series of posts belonging to the same class and occupied simultaneously or in succession by the same individual will appear in the diagram as a single square. Each column is labeled with a number and a letter indicating the social background (in terms of father's profession) and educational history (type of training) of each individual. The code is as follows:

Government Control over Economic Life

1. Head of firm in industry or commerce, banker, corporate director
2. Liberal profession, senior civil servant
3. Manager, engineer, professor
4. Craftsman, small merchant, white-collar worker, middle management, blue-collar worker
A. Polytechnique, Mines, Centrale
B. Institut d'Etudes politiques, Faculté de droit, Ecole des Hautes Etudes Commerciales
C. Primary or secondary school, baccalaureate.

Example: 1B, son of a head of firm who studied at the Institut d'Etudes politiques, the Faculté de droit, or HEC.

From P. Bourdieu, L. Boltanski, M. de Saint-Martin, "Les stratégies de reconversion," *Informations sur les sciences sociales* (October 1973):76-77.

considerable influence in the business world, often control other firms and banks, what we are witnessing is the formation of a cohesive group of individuals exercising influence in politics, business, and the bureaucracy, a group that is also largely homogeneous, owing to the fact that senior bureaucrats play leading roles in all three areas.[36] The effect, then, of the changing strategies of large firms and their growing concentration has been to increase the interpenetration of public and private sectors: where once the government technocracy encouraged modernization from without, now it has joined the modernizing faction in business to work for further changes from within.

In the flow of personnel from the government to private business, the Grands Corps play a leading role. While preserving their distinctive character on the recruitment side, the Grands Corps have been sending a significant fraction of their members to work for big business firms on a temporary or permanent basis, thereby establishing close contact between government leaders and the management of large industrial firms and banks. As table 6.2 shows, under the Fifth Republic most of those leaving the Grands Corps have gone into the private sector. Except for the diplomatic corps, which has traditionally placed members within the administration itself, this tendency has been characteristic in one degree or another of all the Grands Corps under the Fifth Republic.

Thus 54.2 percent of the members of the Conseil d'Etat who leave the corps for a shorter or longer period have gone to work for private firms. The same is true for 58.1 percent of those leaving the Inspection des Finances, for 33.5 percent of those leaving the Cour des comptes, and, finally, for 32.5 percent of those quitting the prefectoral corps.

As under the Third and Fourth Republics, the members of the Grands Corps are eager to transfer to the private sector, where in many cases they hold important jobs in management, thereby strengthening state control of the economy. However, the number of Grands Corps members who leave their corps but remain in the public sector as managers of public or semipublic firms should not be underestimated. Such transfers account for 25.8 percent of those leaving the Conseil d'Etat and 27 percent of those leaving the Inspection des Finances;

TABLE 6.2 "Pantouflage" by Individuals Leaving Grands Corps (1958-74)

Positions Taken (%)	Conseil d'Etat	Inspection des Finances	Cour des comptes	Diplomatic corps	Prefectoral corps
Public firms	13%	16.5%	17%	25%	11.5%
Public firm + board seat in public sector	8.6	10.5	10.6	20	7.8
Board seat in public sector	4.2		5.5		2
Private firm	30.4	30	17.7	10	15
Private firm + board seat in private sector	10.8	24	13.2	10	8.1
Board seat in private sector	13	2			4
Business association		2.1	2.6	5	5.5
SEM	6.5	2	4		7.1
Chair of public commission	6.5	7.3	22.7	5	1.8
Other administration	2.1	2	3	15	27
Intermediary institution		2			

the corresponding figures are 33.1 percent for the Cour des comptes, 45 percent for the diplomatic corps, and, finally, 21.3 percent for the prefectoral corps. Thus transfers within the government are of considerable significance, particularly for the Cour des comptes, the diplomatic corps, and the prefectoral corps. Indeed, if we add to the preceding figures the numbers of those accepting posts as chairmen of public commissions or with another administrative department, we find that 58.8 percent of those leaving the Cour des comptes remain within the public sector; the same is true for 65 percent of those leaving the diplomatic corps and 50.1 percent of those leaving the prefectoral corps.[37] Thus there are two kinds of transfer, the importance of each varying somewhat depending on which corps we are looking at: the first kind of transfer is from government to large firms in the private sector, the second is from the Grands Corps to firms in the public sector or to other centers of power within the government. Recalling, moreover, that large numbers of Grands Corps members have been taking ministerial staff positions and in some cases even becoming ministers themselves, we can begin to appreciate the magnitude of the influence of these homogeneous and cohesive organizations.

Pantouflage and the Banks and Mass Media

We must now look to see where the Grands Corps members seek employment when they move into the public and private business sectors. Right away we notice (table 6.3) that the banking and financial sectors are clearly favored by those leaving not only the Inspection des Finances and the Cour des comptes but also, somewhat more surprisingly, the Conseil d'Etat. In other words, officials leaving the most important corps in the government have headed, often after serving on ministerial staffs, for jobs in the key sector of the contemporary capitalist economy, the sector which increasingly is exerting a controlling influence over the productive apparatus itself. In June 1974, for example, we find five inspecteurs des Finances on the board of directors of the Compagnie financière de Suez and six on the board of the Compagnie financière de Paris et des Pays-Bas.[38]

TABLE 6.3   Sectors Chosen by Senior Bureaucrats, 1958–74

	Conseil d'Etat	Inspection des Finances	Cour des comptes	Diplomatic corps	Prefects
Coal				16.6%	6.4%
Oil		2.2%	5.4%		4.7
Gas					1.7
Electricity	2.7%	3.3	9		4.2
Metals	2.7	2.2	14		1.8
Automobile			5		6.4
Aviation	2.7		2.6		1.8
Transportation	8.1	10.1			18
Construction		4.4			2.8
Regional development	8.1	2.2	2.6	16.6	15.5
Real estate	2.7	2.2	5.4		3.5
Finance	13.5	21.5	25.3	8.3	5.4
Banking	24.3	27	2.6	8.3	2
Insurance	8.1	7.8	6.3		1.8
Publishing, newspapers, radio and TV	13.5		8.1	24.9	14.2
Miscellaneous	13.5	11.3	4.5	16.6	13
Chemicals, pharmaceuticals		3.4	2.6		
Weapons		2.2			

By virtue of their leadership positions in the banking sector, members of the Grands Corps who have gone over to the civilian side control an essential part of the industrial sector. The second area chosen by large numbers of Grands Corps members is that of the mass media, that is, the press, publishing, radio, and so forth. Once again this is a key area for exerting control over civil society, power over the media helping the state to establish the cultural hegemony it needs to justify its legitimacy.[39]

Now that we have had a look at the sectors chosen by bureaucrats leaving the government, it should be interesting to take a closer look at those going into the mass media. Looking at management personnel of selected newspapers, magazines, and radio-TV stations,[40] some seventy-seven persons in all, twelve of whom are not listed in *Who's Who in France,* we very quickly find that former bureaucrats are very much in evidence. Indeed, of the sixty-five persons whose socioprofessional background is known, sixteen had served in the bureaucracy, thirteen of them belonging to the Grands Corps. Of these sixteen individuals (who were particularly prominent within the Hachette publishing house, the radio station Europe 1, and the TV network FR 3), nine had served on a ministerial staff, as had four other individuals from the remainder of the sample, or thirteen in all. Out of a group of sixty-five persons who controlled the key mass media in 1975, then, we find sixteen former civil servants and thirteen individuals who had served on ministerial staffs.

Thus this brief analysis of pantouflage by members of the Grands Corps has shown that the state exerts strong control over key areas of the business world, such as the banks and the mass media. If we recall that bureaucrats from the Grands Corps are also well represented among the heads of the top one hundred French firms, we may assert that the people in control of the bureaucratic apparatus, in many cases the sons of former civil servants, afford the state the means to control all the strategic points in the society.[41]

The Government and Firms in the Public Sector

The foregoing tables have made clear how many members of the Grands Corps took jobs with public-sector firms. It is well known that such firms are an important part of the French economy: indeed, in the areas of coal, gas, electricity, cigarettes, and telecommunications they enjoy a near monopoly. Furthermore, they have an important place in such diverse sectors as aeronautics, weapons systems, construction, the petroleum and automobile industries, and so on. These large public-sector firms are almost always managed by men who have left a Grand Corps but remained within the state sector. Some high officials take such posts to cap off careers in the civil service, while others use them as stepping-stones to jobs in the private sector, and still others come to public industry after a stint on a ministerial staff. M. Dupont-Fauville, for example, chief of staff under Prime Minister Michel Debré, was subsequently named head of the Crédit national; similarly, Pierre Galichon went from General de Gaulle's staff to the presidency of Air France,[42] and, more recently, Claude-Pierre Brossolette left Valéry Giscard d'Estaing's presidential staff to become the head of the Crédit lyonnais.

Unfortunately there exists no systematic study of the management personnel of public-sector firms. Such a study would be of capital importance, for it would help to explain one of the means by which the state controls a key sector of the economy, analogous to the way top bureaucrats exert strong influence over private business. Nevertheless, preliminary analysis of a limited sample of public and semipublic firms has provided some information about the personnel who manage them.[43] The firms selected were all public-sector firms occupying key positions in various areas of the economy: RATP (mass transportation), EDF (public utility), EMC, Renault (automobiles), FORMA (agriculture), RFP, SNCF (railroad), CFP (oil), Havas (press), SNIAS (aerospace). The study examined the presidents, general managers, and board members of these firms, 103 persons in all.

In many cases sons of civil servants, most of these individuals had studied political science and law; 17 of them had attended the ENA, a very high proportion given that this school is relatively new. Of the 103 individuals, 77 were civil servants, 44 of them members of an administrative or technical Grand Corps; furthermore, 16 of the civil servants (including 8 members of the Grands Corps) had transferred into private firms, and these were joined by 17 company presidents and board members whose only experience was in the private sector. Once again, therefore, we find the same close connection between the civil service and the world of business that we found earlier when we looked at the industrialization commissions, though here business is less well represented.

The main point to notice is the degree to which these large public-sector firms are controlled by senior civil servants, who often use political experience as a springboard to a management position. Thirty-one individuals in the sample had worked on ministerial staffs, and twenty-four others took part in commissions or councils named by the executive: public-sector firms are virtually a part of the government apparatus itself. Like giant firms in the private sector, public firms of national scope are thus managed by a small group of men, homogeneous in their origins and experienced in politics, business, and administration, always at the highest levels of responsibility. It would seem, then, that these public-sector firms offer especially good opportunities for contact among leaders in these three different areas. Since these firms are often strategically placed in their sectors, they may be regarded as links between the government and business.[44] The Fifth Republic has seen close integration of the various centers of power: this has been accomplished mainly thanks to the mobility of senior civil servants, who move from top spot to top spot in each particular area.

7 The Giscardian System
The Impossible Fusion of Power and the Decline of State Autonomy

The immediate consequence of Valéry Giscard d'Estaing's election as president of the Republic was to bring to power a fresh group of political leaders, many of whom were members of the Independent Republican movement. The governmental apparatus built up by the UDR was dismantled, and the new government entered into a different kind of relationship with certain social groups. Before we attempt to show the distinctive character of the Giscardian government's relations with, say, businessmen, it is well to look at the new faces that took control of the party.

The new president was not bound by the cronyism that had been so influential during the Gaullist years; added to this was the fact that the generation of leaders who had participated in the Resistance was on its way out. The Gaullist barons who had clung to power under the presidency of Georges Pompidou were now excluded from responsibility: Pierre Messmer, Roger Frey, Maurice Couve de Murville, Michel Debré, Louis Joxe, E. Michelet, André Malraux, and R. Capitant suddenly vanished from the political scene. Henceforth the Independent Republicans were in power, and on their coattails were the "young Turks" of the UDR, anxious to hold on to power and aware that they were still indispensable, since they alone could keep the UDR's parliamentary contingent, which supported the presidential majority in the National Assembly, in line.

Giscardism and the Mutation of the Independent Republicans

To understand what is distinctive about Giscardism, we must look into the origins of the movement. Residuary legatee of the Centre national des indépendants (CNI) of the

Fourth Republic, itself a part of the "Orleanist"[1] wing of the moderate right led by Antoine Pinay, the Independent Republicans (RI) grew out of a split in the CNI in 1962. This rift originated in conflicting positions on the war in Algeria, with the Independent Republicans accepting the Gaullist policy rejected by the overwhelming majority of the CNI. Following the 1962 legislative elections, an RI group took shape within the National Assembly. Allies of the UDR, the Independent Republicans, led by Valéry Giscard d'Estaing, aimed to create a modern right-wing movement unfettered by ties to the extreme right and the OAS, which would be able to serve as a political nucleus in the post-Gaullist era.

The National Federation of Independent Republicans became a reality in 1966 after Giscard's departure from the finance ministry. It took upon itself the explicit task of unifying the moderate right. The membership of the RI at this time consisted largely of notables with strong local roots. In this respect they differed markedly from the Gaullist deputies, many of whom could claim no particular local prestige. The leadership of the federation during this period reflected this characteristic of the parliamentary party. The *président-delégué* was Raymond Mondon, son of a wine-grower and a lawyer by profession. He had enjoyed a long political career under the Fourth Republic and was mayor of Metz and a member of the *conseil général*. Thus he fitted the description of the traditional political professional. Similarly, the leadership in 1966 also included Marcel Anthonioz, son of a public works contractor and a hotelkeeper by profession, not a university graduate, mayor of Divonne-les-Bains, member of the conseil général since 1945, elected deputy in 1951, and president of the national association of tourist hotels; R. Marcellin, a lawyer, deputy for Morbihan since 1945, secretary of state (i.e., a junior minister) under the Fourth Republic, conseiller général since 1953, president of the Morbihan conseil général in 1964, and destined to be elected senator from Morbihan in 1974; Robert Boscary-Monservin, a lawyer, farmer, mayor, deputy for Aveyron since 1958, to be elected senator in 1971; Jean Chamant, lawyer, deputy for Yonne since 1946, secretary of state under the Fourth Republic, destined to become president of the conseil régional of Burgundy in 1973; André

Bettencourt, a lawyer's son who did not attend university, conseiller général for the canton of Lillebonne since 1946, mayor, deputy for Seine-Maritime (1951), secretary of state under the Fourth Republic, and destined to become president of the conseil régional of Haute-Normandie in 1974; Aimé Paquet, a farmer and farmer's son who did not attend university, conseiller général since 1945, mayor in 1947, deputy for Isère since 1951; only Jean de Broglie, son of a wealthy owner of timberland and conseiller général since 1941, had served with the Conseil d'Etat.

Thus when Valéry Giscard d'Estaing founded the National Federation of Independent Republicans, he surrounded himself for the most part with professional politicians. Lawyers in many cases, frequently sons of lawyers or rural landowners, the early Giscardians often had not attended university; they held many local offices which they had been cultivating since the early days of the Fourth Republic, in which many of them had served as ministers. When later eased out of power, these professional politicians managed to hold on to or acquire important local offices, such as the presidency of a conseil régional, which symbolized their power as important local figures with deep roots in the community. Thus the individuals in control of the Independent Republicans at this time had nothing to do with the senior civil servants who were in total control of the executive under the Fifth Republic. In a "Republic of functionaries" they were notables who seemingly belonged to another era. Not a single vice-president of the RI in 1966 had graduated from the ENA and subsequently pursued a career in the civil service; moreover, the party leadership was completely cut off from the world of big business and the large, concentrated firms associated with the modernizing capitalist spirit. Accordingly, the Giscardian Independent Republicans seemed a thousand miles from the centers of national power: they were basically powerful local notables.

After the legislative elections of April 1967, there was a change in the leadership of the RI, which had undergone a profound transformation. Although R. Mondon remained vice-president, all the former regional vice-presidents were either demoted to the status of mere members of the leadership committee or eliminated altogether. As committee members, they were joined by Charles Hardy, son of an industrialist, ENA graduate, subprefect, and member of Valéry Giscard d'Estaing's staff as finance minister, and Xavier de la Fournière, a dealer in foreign exchange with connections to industry. Thus industry and the civil service had gained a foothold on the leadership committee of the Independent Republicans. Moreover, Michel Poniatowski and Paul Dijoud became secretary-general and assistant secretary-general, respectively. Both foreshadowed the new Giscardian personnel who would gradually take over the RI. They were ENA graduates who had close ties to big business and ministerial staff experience (Poniatowski had been Giscard's chief of staff at Finances). Finally, Roger Chinaud, son of a senior civil servant, industrialist, experienced in the administration, became political secretary of the new party committee, which differed markedly from the old one in that it was staffed by people with backgrounds identical to those in power under the UDR government. From this time forward the influence of the rural notables diminished greatly in relation to that of senior civil servants whose collaboration was indispensable if the RI hoped at a later date to become a party of government.

Next came an organizational effort that resulted in a restructuring of the party apparatus on the local as well as the national level, coupled with a relentless campaign to influence public opinion that was a foretaste of the campaign for the presidency; after the 1968 legislative elections, the RI acquired yet another new leadership committee. This time, all the traditional politicians were gone. In place of the local notables, senior civil servants took over all the leadership posts. The vice-presidential spot hitherto occupied by Raymond Mondon was eliminated, while Michel Poniatowski's was retained. Along with Paul Dijoud, new members of the RI leadership included J.-P. Soisson, son of an industrialist, ENA graduate, and member of several ministerial staffs; Michel d'Ornano, son of an industrialist and an industrialist himself; and V. Chapot, former chief of staff under Giscard (1959), who would again become chief of staff in 1969 before being named trésorier-payeur général in 1970.

This time "the end of the notables" was lasting: a new group of politician-bureaucrats was formed for the purpose of taking control of the government away from the group then in power, which in certain respects resembled the new group quite closely. Of the eleven persons in the party leadership, five were ENA graduates, and there were men who had served on ministerial staffs and industrialists whose fathers were either civil servants or industrialists. In order to move from the status of a minority faction within the majority to that of a governing party, the RI chose leaders apt to fill future government posts. In doing so they moved away from the traditional moderate right, the notables with strong local roots who stood aloof from economic modernization and had no affinity with those currently in power. The technocratic right supplanted the notables ensconced in their local fiefdoms.

The percentage of senior civil servants in the RI's parliamentary contingent increased noticeably, from 6 percent in 1958 to 18 percent in 1968, surpassing the Gaullists in this respect; from this time on the RI had the highest proportion of senior civil servants of any party. In 1968, moreover, the proportion of industrialists rose considerably, slightly exceeding that of the UDR.[2] On the other hand, there were more landowners in the RI than in the UDR, though the percentage fell a good deal, from 22 percent in 1958 to 15 percent in 1968, compared with 4.5 percent for the UDR. Large landowners were gradually replaced by senior civil servants, though the former continued to play a significant role in the RI, unlike in the UDR, which was clearly more of a popular party and had virtually no representation of landed wealth. The UDR, for example, could boast of a small percentage of blue- and white-collar workers in its ranks,[3] whereas the RI had none at all.

Furthermore, the RI deputies have for two generations been drawn mainly from the most privileged strata of society, whereas many UDR deputies come from more modest social backgrounds.[4] In addition, Giscardian deputies are more likely to have noble ancestors than are UDR deputies (11 nobles out of 58 deputies among the RI, 14 out of 291 for the UDR).[5] Ideologically, the RI deputies are happy to identify themselves as members of the right wing, while their UDR colleagues are loath to do so; some RI deputies began their political careers with the Leagues in the interwar period, and compared with the UDR only half as many participated in the Resistance.⁶ Finally, while many UDR deputies owe their election to the Gaullist label and lack local power bases, almost all RI deputies were first elected to local offices thanks to the prestige they enjoyed as notables even before serving in parliament.

These differences were perpetuated by the 1973 legislative elections: 6 percent of the UDR deputies were blue- and white-collar workers, groups almost completely absent among the RI; 46 percent of UDR deputies were salaried employees, as against only 29 percent for the RI.⁷ On the other hand, 20 percent of the Independent Republicans headed industrial or commercial firms, and 16 percent were farmers, almost all of them large landowners. In the 1973 elections, then, the moderate right was fundamentally distinct from the Gaullists, who in keeping with their ideology tried to represent all classes of French society. In the 1974 presidential elections, this difference was readily apparent: "the most conservative segment of the old majority was joined by virtually all the 'centrist' voters of March 1973."⁸ Thus in both the legislative and presidential elections, the Giscardian voters stood out in contrast to the Gaullist voters.

The changes in the RI's parliamentary contingent, however, were less significant than the changes in the federation's leadership committee: among the committee members there were no longer any of the local notables or farmers who still figured in large numbers in the parliamentary party and who, among the voters, consciously chose to support the Giscardians; while the number of civil servants in the parliamentary party was increasing slowly, in the leadership committee they achieved overwhelming supremacy. The differences between parliament and the political leadership that are characteristic, as we have seen, of the Fifth Republic as a whole, are again in evidence, though in attenuated form, in the RI. The party leadership, far more than the parliamentary party, was dominated by senior civil servants and industrialists interested in economic development.

If we look now at Giscardian ministers, we find these differences accentuated still further. In this connection, it is interesting to compare RI ministers who were appointed during the presidencies of General de Gaulle and Georges Pompidou with those who took office under Giscard. We find an evolution that parallels the evolution of the party leadership as described above. Among the ministers, the decline of local notables is even more pronounced than in the leadership committee: de Gaulle and Pompidou appointed such notables, but they were quickly eased out of power by Giscard, who preferred to name former bureaucrats from his own party.

Independent Republican ministers named by de Gaulle and Pompidou included M. Anthonioz, A. Bettencourt, C. Bonnet, J. Chamant, R. Mondon, J.-L. Tinaud, V. Giscard d'Estaing, J. de Broglie, M. Poniatowski, A. Paquet, R. Marcellin, and P. Dijoud. All were members of the RI leadership committee in 1966. As noted previously, Mondon, Anthonioz, Bettencourt, de Broglie, Chamant, and Marcellin were all traditional notables who held a number of elective offices and for the most part were engaged in professions characteristic of the professional politician. Except for Giscard, the others—Poniatowski and Dijoud—entered the party leadership in 1967 when most of the notables were stripped of their power. These two were the only ones who continued as ministers under Giscard: in other words, the ministers who were civil servants stayed in power when the presidency changed hands, while the ministers who were local notables either quit the political arena or pursued careers as senators or local officials far from the central authority of the executive.[9]

For further confirmation of this transformation of the RI leadership, we may look to the list of ministers from the party appointed under Giscard's presidency. Besides the three men who had served in earlier governments—Poniatowski, Dijoud, and Bonnet—we find M. Cavaillé, B. Destremeau, H. Dorlhac, G. Ducray, J.-P. Fourcade, M. d'Ornano, J.-P. Soisson, and P.-C. Taittinger. Some of these men are ENA graduates and civil servants (Fourcade, Soisson, Destremeau), who joined other civil-servant ministers remaining from previous governments. Fourcade left the ENA to become inspecteur des Finances, was appointed to Giscard's staff (1959-61), became directeur général du Commerce et des Prix, transferred to the private sector as head of the Société d'épargne immobilière and member of the board of the Banque transatlantique, and, finally, was named minister, though he had never been a deputy; he had no local power base until 1971, when he became mayor of Saint Cloud. Similarly, Jean-Pierre Soisson graduated from the ENA and joined the Cour des comptes, is the son of an industrialist, served on ministerial staffs under the Fifth Republic, and became a deputy in 1968. B. Destremeau is the son of a general and a career diplomat; he has been a deputy only since 1967 and has no local power base. Thus these senior civil servants are quite unlike traditional notables and markedly different from the usual political professional.

Besides the senior civil servants, many of whom have connections with big business, some men who were themselves businessmen served in the Chirac government. Among them were Michel d'Ornano, son of an industrialist and an industrialist himself who contributed to the economic development of his region and served as president of CODER-Normandie, and P.-C. Taittinger, similarly son of a businessman and himself a businessman, president of the Lutétia and Concorde hotels, chairman of the board of Taittinger champagnes, of the Banque de l'Union occidentale, and Ripolin. Once in power, the Independent Republican party was radically transformed in order to fill its governmental role: to that end it recruited civil servants and businessmen with a zeal hitherto unmatched, clearly in consequence of Giscard's overall policy, which focused basically on problems of the economy and tended to neglect traditional political concerns.

This policy orientation emerges with still greater clarity if we look at the socioprofessional background of ministers who were not members of either the UDR, the CDS, or the Radical party, that is, ministers without explicit party affiliation but loyal to Giscardism—modernist, technocratic, and liberal. Almost all of these men were drawn from the ranks of the civil service, and many of them had participated in the administration of economic affairs. One such is Raymond Barre, a graduate in law, Jeanneney's chief of staff at the Ministry of Industry and Commerce, Common Market functionary, and member of the board of governors of the Banque de France. He had never held elective office. Nor had Lionel Stoleru, another expert on economic matters, graduate of the Ecole Polytechnique, and son of an industrialist, who worked for the Commissariat Général du Plan before taking a management position with the Crédit lyonnais and later joining Giscard's staff at the finance ministry. Both men, then, are important technocrats who have never had to deal with political problems; they are the antithesis of the typical minister or deputy of the Third and Fourth Republics, and their presence in the government is indicative of the advent of politicians with a new outlook, bent on governing society scientifically. In the Gaullist "Republic of functionaries" these men strengthened the Saint-Simonian tendencies of the regime. Now, it seems, the "Republic of functionaries" has given way to a "Republic of economists," some of whose ministers have been drawn directly from industry, others from the civil service after "pantouflage" in the private sector, and still others from among government economic specialists.

In the same vein, mention may be made of Jean François-Poncet, son of an ambassador, former student of the ENA and of Harvard, who transferred to the private sector where he served as head of Carnaud and Forges de Basse-Indre (part of the De Wendel conglomerate), and who, like many of his colleagues, was never elected deputy prior to being appointed minister; or, again, André Postel-Vinay, inspecteur des Finances and later banker. In this connection, we should point out that a rather large number of ministers have served at one point or another in their careers in the banking sector, whether public or private: in addition to J.-P. Fourcade and André Postel-Vinay, we can point to Lionel Stoleru and Raymond Barre himself. It is beyond doubt, then, that more Giscardian than Gaullist ministers have held positions in banking and industry. And these Giscardian ministers have had the help of senior civil servants brought in to fill positions of authority from high administrative posts, who, like their colleagues, never served as deputies before being named ministers.[10]

The ministers without avowed party affiliation share with their Independent Republican colleagues the ambition to run their ministries in a technocratic and scientific manner. Neither those with nor those without party affiliation are notables, and most of them have never been elected deputies; this has caused an even wider gulf to develop between parliament and the executive. In this respect, the Giscardian ministers are more like those appointed under de Gaulle's presidency than under Pompidou's. As noted previously, General de Gaulle's civil-servant ministers—such as W. Baumgartner, L. Joxe, L. Paye, P. Guillaumat, B. Chenot, and P. Chatenet— were not deputies before becoming ministers, and except for Louis Joxe did not enter parliament after leaving their ministries. Similarly, J.-P. Fourcade, J. Sauvagnargues, S. Veil, M. Bigeard, L. Stoleru, J. François-Poncet, R. Barre, R. Haby, and A. Saunier-Seïté are all senior civil servants who were never deputies. By contrast, under the Pompidou system, O. Stirn, J.-P. Lecat, A. Peyrefitte, J. Chirac, J. Charbonnel, and others were civil servants who were elected deputies before being appointed ministers: Pompidou's attempt to bring government closer to civil society meant that ministers who were civil servants should seek to build a political base and legitimize their power through the ballot box. Compared with the situation in the Pompidou regime, the distance between the politico-administrative apparatus and parliament was greater under de Gaulle and is again greater under Giscard.

Indeed, under Giscard the importance of the traditional career path that once led from local office to parliament and on to a ministry has declined steadily. In the Chirac government 45.94 percent of the ministers went directly from a ministerial staff post to nomination as minister, and 16.20 percent from parliament to the government; by contrast, between January 1959 and June 1974, that is, during the presidencies of de Gaulle and Pompidou, these proportions were 36.1 percent and 26 percent respectively.[11] Giscardian ministers often avoid parliament, then: they are mainly senior civil servants who have served on ministerial staffs and in many cases have spent time working in industry or banking.[12]

The Staffs of Valéry Giscard d'Estaing and Jacques Chirac

If Enarchs—as ENA-trained technocrats are known—were numerous in the Chirac government, they are still more numerous on the staff of President Valéry Giscard d'Estaing: ten of the eighteen staff members are ENA graduates. This is the highest percentage on any presidential or prime ministerial staff in the Fifth Republic.[13] Unlike ministers in the Chirac government, who, if they were civil servants, had often worked briefly in business before returning to the government, or who were themselves industrialists and sometimes sons of industrialists, the members of Giscard's staff are senior civil servants who have not worked in the private sector, preferring to remain in their specialized roles in the government.[14]

In contrast to ministers in the Chirac government, then, the members of the presidential staff have stood aloof from the private sector; nor are there any traditional politicians on the staff, while there are a few among the ministers, such as Jean Lecanuet. Unlike the composition of the government, which is the result of political compromises among the various groups within the majority and of the necessity to adapt to the requirements of universal suffrage, the composition of the presidential staff signifies above all the president's desire to forge his own instrument of action: this accounts for the exclusion of men connected with business or traditional politics. In this respect, too, Giscardism is similar to Gaullism, the president surrounding himself with civil servants whose skills he can use to advance his own policies.

A further difference between the president's staff and that of his former prime minister is that the latter included political advisers mainly concerned with campaign strategy. Thus Pierre Juillet and Marie-France Garaud were assigned the task of consolidating political gains and holding on to provincial support, as well as conveying to the leadership the wishes of rank-and-file UDR deputies who had no access to the president.

These two political advisers had earlier played the same role on Pompidou's presidential staff: close to the UDR rank-and-file at the time, and to such young Turks as Jacques Chirac, they were hostile to the technocratic liberalism then prevalent at the Matignon* and made their hostility known by attacking the policies of Jacques Chaban-Delmas [then prime minister] in the name of the basically conservative bedrock of the electorate. Now, under Chirac, they represented the interests of the political class, which made its voice heard within the majority by loudly refusing to support the law on capital gains and by its opposition to "permissive morals." In 1976, however, Pierre Juillet and Marie-France Garaud

---

*The prime minister's office.—Trans.

were members of the staff of their friend of long standing, Jacques Chirac, who was then prime minister; they were no longer as in the Pompidou era at the Elysée, where the real power lay. What is more, within the Chirac government itself they ran up against the opposition of the Independent Republican ministers, who, as civil servants and industrialists, were a long way from sharing the concerns of provincial France, expressed through the UDR rank and file. It was no longer possible to thwart the implementation of Chaban-style liberalism, favoring concentration of big businesses and a rigorous policy of free competition that worked against small firms—not from the Matignon, when the decisions were taken at the Elysée and backed up by the Independent Republican ministers and their allies in the Chirac government.

Thus the technocrats, most of them ENA graduates and members of the Grands Corps, resembled one another, spoke a common language, and shared the same culture, but they supported divergent economic policies and defended different political interests on behalf of antagonistic social groups. Senior civil servants had indeed moved into the top spots in the government and forced out the professional politicians: this does not mean, however, that they all behaved politically in the same way. Many Independent Republican civil servants became ministers after serving on ministerial staffs without being elected deputies; they displayed little sensitivity to the wishes of *la France profonde,* with which they had few direct contacts. By contrast, under Pompidou civil servants became ministers after being elected deputies, and showed much greater awareness of the concerns of provincial France; they had close ties with rank-and-file deputies and identified with classical radicalism, sharing the fears of the middle classes and the provincial petty bourgeoisie in the face of a rapid modernization of the economy which worked to the advantage of big business.

Thus within the government Giscardism has coexisted with Pompidolism: each has the support of a group of civil servants and defends the interests of social groups antagonistic to those defended by the other, though for the time being they remain allies. Brief mention of the economic policies backed by the Giscardians is enough, however, to reveal the width of the gulf that separates the two: the law on capital gains, which had no effect on large corporations but fell squarely on the middle classes, is one example among other.

The Giscardian "Breeding Ground": The "Perspectives et Réalité" Clubs

To carry out its economic policies, Giscardism had need of political agents who shared its vision of things and who could spread that vision with sufficient fervor to persuade the electorate and alter the existing composition of the parliamentary majority by bringing large numbers of Giscardian deputies into office in the 1978 legislative elections. In 1965 Valéry Giscard d'Estaing founded the "Perspectives et Réalité" clubs, some 218 of which are in existence throughout France today, with a combined membership of 40,000. This movement was organized outside the Independent Republican party: no party deputy, for example, held a seat on the steering committee elected on February 7, 1976. The purpose of these clubs was to bring together people who for the most part had no party affiliation, thereby drumming up support for the new presidential majority. They played an important role in the 1974 presidential elections in providing Giscard's candidacy with a grass-roots organization.

The clubs are carefully organized meeting-places designed to influence not the traditional notables, much less the workers, but rather management personnel, industrialists, civil servants, and professionals. The support of these socioprofessional groups is needed to back up the changes already made in the Independent Republican party. The clubs are aimed at attracting social groups which have shown themselves to favor fundamental economic changes in France and which are often eager to move away from Gaullism, which they find metaphysical, irrational, sometimes populist, and in any case impossible to identify with. Enamored of rationality, these socioprofessional groups can support the Giscardian political formula, the cult of nonpartisan competence.

This formula is the basis of Giscardian ideology; it showed how effective it could be in the 1974 televised presidential debate between Giscard and [Socialist candidate] François Mitterrand, during which Giscard sought to portray himself as the embodiment of scientific competence, which alone could quell the purely ideological excesses of an essentially partisan left, while at the same time supplanting a sometimes metaphysical Gaullism. In Giscard's view, "progress" makes possible "development" and therefore economic "growth," which benefits all groups in French society.[15]

All the publications of the clubs are imbued with this view of politics. Accordingly, the monthly *Perspectives et Réalité* devotes most of its analyses to economic growth, the guarantor of progress, to rational ways of fighting inflation, and to means of developing foreign trade. It was not by chance that Jean-Pierre Fourcade, symbol of the efficiency-oriented Giscardism of the dynamic Enarchs, a man who had moved from government to business and back to government again, employing talents and concepts equally applicable to both public and private domains, was elected president of the Perspectives et Réalité clubs. As an expert well versed in economics, Fourcade offers his monthly reflections on rational economic approaches to the nation's problems in each issue of the clubs' magazine. In his editorials, as in most of the articles published by this journal, politics rarely figures explicitly: instead, the inspecteurs des Finances who write many of the articles analyze in learned style the problems associated with development and regulated economic growth, about which they would have us believe they are in sole possession of the pertinent scientific expertise.

Thus relays of economics experts relentlessly set forth the view, page after page, that expansion neutralizes social conflict and thereby preserves the freedom of all. Conflict is stripped of its structural character and said to become easier to avoid as time goes by. It is therefore not difficult to understand that Michel Poniatowski should have been "enchanted" by Jean Fourastié's courses in economics,[16] which also take the view that industrialization promotes social peace. The "enlightened" bourgeoisie looks to the future with hope: it sees in science and technology the means to organize society on a rational basis and to hasten harmonious growth.

The vocabulary used is an optimistic one, which ignores structural conflict, claims to be scientifically neutral, and may be seen as the latest avatar of the "end of ideology" school that has wreaked such havoc in the social sciences.[17] In the optimistic vision of the Giscardians, an adequate mastery of management techniques will make possible evolution without revolution in the economy and modernization without conflict in French society: change by consensus.[18] Economics will replace politics and science will drive out useless ideologies. This explains the fascination with economics that is prevalent in the Perspectives et Réalité clubs, most of whose working sessions are devoted to the study of economic questions.

Since we have no information about the socioprofessional background of the club membership, we can do no more than examine the composition of the present steering committee. Unfortunately we have been unable to obtain biographical information about all the steering committee members, as some of them are not listed in any directory. Information was available on only twenty-six individuals, and this may have produced a somewhat distorted image of the committee, since those on whom no information was available were probably supervisory and office personnel not covered by *Who's Who* and other biographical listings. Looking at the twenty-six individuals on whom information was available, we find that ten were owners or presidents of companies in industry or commerce and two were officials of the CNPF; the rest were mainly senior civil servants belonging to the Grands Corps (two inspecteurs des Finances) or working for departments of the central government (four) or in higher education (three). In addition to these two groups, there were also doctors, lawyers, and managers; doubtless there would have been more of the latter had we been able to find information on the twenty-one missing individuals. These are the socioprofessional groups from which politicians have traditionally sprung.

The point to notice is that the Giscardians have deliberately turned to these "breeding grounds" (as the Perspectives et Réalité clubs refer to themselves) to recruit new personnel from a membership composed on the one hand of industrialists and senior civil servants and, on the other hand, of managers and professional men. Furthermore, many of the industrialists on the steering committee come from such advanced sectors of the economy as chemicals, electricity, gas, metals, mass media, and insurance, while managers are drawn from both big business and the PME. Thus the steering committee, it should be noted, includes representatives of big business favorably disposed toward the liberal policies adopted by the Giscardians to hasten industrial concentration.

Furthermore, some of the twenty-six members counted have political responsibilities: two are ministers or secretaries of state, four are chiefs of ministerial staffs, six are technical advisers, one is an economic adviser, three are mayors of large cities, and two are officials of the Independent Republican party. Once again, therefore, we find a grouping peculiarly characteristic of Giscardism, combining top government officials with representatives of business and industry.

The grip of leading politico-administrative personnel on these clubs may be seen even more clearly if we look at the way they are run. At the top are two Enarchs, both of whom served on Giscard's staff at the finance ministry. In addition, the predecessor of the present secretary-general is also an ENA graduate and also worked on Giscard's staff. As we have noted on several occasions, Giscard's various staffs have been prime springboards to leadership roles for Giscardian politicians.[19]

Finally, the new leadership's control over the clubs may be seen in the way they are run: clubs are constantly visited by civil servants, almost all of whom work on the staffs of Independent Republican ministers or other ministers closely allied with the Giscardians and not connected with the UDR, who come to deliver the good word, that is, to preach the virtues of economic science, which is supposed to allow the reconciliation of liberalism with harmonious growth. In this regard, reading the "club life" section in each month's *Perspectives et Réalité* is instructive: in each issue there are announcements of visits by staff members, the topics they discuss, and so forth. In particular, the members of the staff of one-time finance minister Jean-Pierre Fourcade figure prominently in these club meetings, often traveling in regiments as experts in economic science: in the clubs' economics seminar in November 1975, for example, along with officials of other ministries six of Fourcade's staff members took part in the working sessions of this Giscardian "breeding ground." As president of the clubs, Fourcade saw to it that his staff was constantly on the move in the provinces, along with members of Michel Poniatowski's staff: they ran meetings of local clubs which subprefects in the area did not deign to attend. Besides ministerial staff members who gave unstintingly of themselves in these efforts to train the new Giscardian politicians for their future role in parliament, the ministers themselves found time to travel frequently in the provinces for the purpose of promoting new clubs. Once or twice each month Jean-Pierre Fourcade participated in the meeting of a provincial club: he was the leading figure in the club movement and carried the presidential word directly to the provinces. Other ministers close to the Giscardian movement, such as Norbert Segard, Simone Veil, and Helen Dorlhac (a member of the steering committee), did not hesitate to travel to the provinces to assist in the training of the new politicians, who were taught how to handle economic theory and inspired with confidence in the virtues of techniques they looked upon as neutral, apolitical, and effective.

The Giscardian Wager

Not supported by an organized and highly structured party, such as the UDR, or by the large massed-based parties of the French left, Giscardism took for its first task the thorough transformation of the Independent Republican movement within whose womb it had matured. In short order the Giscardians, whose goal was to become the dominant faction within the majority and to stop always playing second fiddle to the Gaullist party, moved to replace the independent notables of the moderate right wing, who had strong local power bases but remained for the most part on the fringes of industrialized and meritocratic France, with senior bureaucrats and industrialists in favor of modernization and concentration of the productive apparatus, changes that must inevitably come at the expense of the bedrock France so dear to the notables and the PME.

After winning the presidency without the help of a solid local organization, the Independent Republicans had no cohesive political movement to back them up and remained by a considerable margin in the minority in parliament. This explains why the Perspectives et Réalité clubs were created for the purpose of hastily mustering a contingent of Giscardian politicians ready to run in the 1978 legislative elections under the presidential banner. Created in the image of the ministers appointed by the president of the Republic, this new party seems to have drawn its recruits mainly from the civil service and the world of business.

In doing so, the Giscardian system seemed to be turning away from the Gaullist model. As long as that model was adhered to, the distinctive role of the high civil service was maintained, enhancing the autonomy of a "Republic of functionaries" concerned, as the Gaullist slogan had it, to assert its "independence" of both foreign influence and the pressure of various domestic socioeconomic groups. Under Gaullism, the state used its bureaucracy to extend its control over civil society: not only was capital unable to coopt the high administration and thereby induce the state to defend its social and economic interests;[20] what is more, senior civil servants seemed to abstain from any participation in business affairs. They remained within the government, moving from the Grands Corps to ministerial staffs and in some cases to ministerial appointments, lending their services to planning efforts not without influence over the economic life of the nation. The Gaullist state's claim to independence rested on the distinctive role of its senior functionaries, through whom it was able to carry out its own policies. If a senior civil servant did transfer to the private sector, he did so upon quitting government service, thereby leaving intact the autonomy of the civil service personnel.

Under Giscard's system, in contrast, many senior civil servants in powerful government positions are closely connected with industry; what is more, some of them have left government for a time to work in private industry before returning to take up, say, a ministerial portfolio alongside colleagues recruited from the world of industry. The "Republic of functionaries" has apparently run its course: it has been replaced by an alliance between bureaucrats and industrialists. In this respect, political, economic, and administrative powers in France have been unified more effectively than at any time since the inception of the Third Republic, which ushered in a period during which the various centers of power were widely separated from one another. The Gaullist "Republic of functionaries" had successfully unified the government and the bureaucracy, however, and now the world of business has been integrated as well.

This renewed unity has translated itself into a liberal economic policy advantageous, as we have seen, to large, concentrated firms; another consequence has been a virtual halt to state planning, the implications of which have already been discussed. Economic liberalism has also meant a sudden halt to Gaullism's "nationalist" economic policy and a rapprochement with large multinational firms, particularly American companies. As industry minister Michel d'Ornano has said, France must "associate with a powerful foreign partner in order to gain access to the market on the best possible terms." The new economic policy of Giscardian devising has already been translated into reality. Examples worthy of mention are the scrapping of a national policy on computers and the change in nuclear policy. In the computer industry, the formation of CII was the impetus behind a national program for computer manufacturing under the so-called "computation plan," involving a partnership among the state, CGE, and Thomson; the founding of Unidata in 1973 made it possible to preserve the broad outlines of this scheme, thanks to a partnership arrangement with foreign firms such as Siemens and Philips, but this ultimately aroused the hostility of participating French firms. In 1975-76 the agreements broke down, and the firm CII-Honeywell-Bull was formed by merger on July 1, 1976.

Thus the unified power structure of the Giscardian system sanctioned the abandonment of a national policy on computers, for it seems that the French have little say on the committee responsible for setting CII-Honeywell-Bull policy. Similarly, the scrapping of one French foray into the nuclear industry deserves brief mention. As late as 1973 the national nuclear policy had been supported by EDF,* which ordered equipment from CGE; but in 1974 the government decided to send some of its orders to Framatome, part of the Empain-

*A publicly owned utility.—Trans.

Westinghouse conglomerate that also controlled Jeumont-Schneider and Creusot-Loire. Then in 1975-76 the policy of diversification was scrapped and the final order went to Framatome.

These examples, chosen from among many similar ones, illustrate the abandonment of Gaullism's "nationalist" pretensions. The point we wish to make here is that this change in policy can be seen reflected in personnel changes in top government posts. Thus the trend of personnel changes is seen, as we maintained at the beginning of this work, to be a significant variable that should be analyzed in its own right and not dismissed disdainfully on the pretext that the correct methodology for the study of society is an atomistic one, giving precedence to the study of individual actors over the study of social phenomena in themselves.

If, by chance, Giscardism should succeed, with the help of the Perspectives et Réalité clubs, in winning a majority in the 1978 legislative elections,* the mutation of the RI would be brought into relief, and for the first time in a long while some measure of socioprofessional and cultural homogeneity would be restored between the parliamentary majority and the government. Gradually the distance that has separated ministers from deputies under the Fifth Republic would be whittled away: the resulting situation would be identical to that which prevailed under the Third and Fourth Republics, in that minsters and deputies would, but for a few minor differences, share a common background and outlook.

In contrast to the Third and Fourth Republics, however—regimes characterized by severe separation of powers in which traditional political professionals held a near monopoly of posts in the government—the Fifth Republic would, if the trend continues, put an end to the privileged position of the politicians and elevate in their stead bureaucrats, industrialists, and senior management personnel. Homogeneity would be reestablished, but the winners would be the socioprofessional groups in control of the administration and in close contact with the powers-that-be in the world of business. The classical parliamentary regime would then be supplanted by a highly

*This did not happen.—Trans.

unified system the likes of which France has not seen since the first half of the nineteenth century. The unity of the regime would embrace the political, administrative, and economic spheres. While the unification effected by Gaullism was limited to the high administration and the executive, thereby protecting the machinery of government against both local influence conveyed through parliament and economic special interests with respect to which, as to civil society in general, the state claimed to maintain independence, the system Giscard would like to see established would put an end to the independence of the state and threaten even its mere autonomy.

Such, at any rate, is the general tendency that lies behind Giscardism's ambitions. In this regard the government reshuffle in late August 1976 illustrates the consolidation of Giscardian influence, placing in relief certain features of Giscardism already revealed by our analysis. Notice first of all the increased number of Giscardians in the Barre government: ten ministers and secretaries of state now claimed affiliation with the "presidential majority," along with ten others belonging to the RI. As against this group of twenty, the UDR was reduced to only nine cabinet members: Giscardization of the government progressed, while the UDR's grip on the majority was weakened.

If we now look at the socioprofessional origins and career background of the seven individuals who entered the government, we find further evidence of a transformation of the ministerial personnel carried out at the expense of the traditional notables, who represented a stagnant France. The three new appointees belonging to the presidential majority were all senior civil servants: besides ambassador Louis de Guiringaud, Christian Beullac and Maurice Ligot are worthy of special mention, since they typify the radical changes in the Independent Republican leadership described above. Both are graduates of Grandes Ecoles, the Ecole Polytechnique and the ENA, respectively. Both are senior civil servants concerned mainly with the solution of economic problems. Of the three, only Ligot had been elected deputy before becoming a minister. Thus all the characteristics noted in our analysis of Giscardism are in evidence.[21]

Conservely, the new appointees belonging to the UDR were not the ENA graduates and civil servants once so numerous among Gaullist ministers, now to be found increasingly in the ranks of the RI. The two major figures among them, Olivier Guichard and Robert Boulin, were above all Gaullists experienced in the world of politics: neither had attended the Grandes Ecoles or worked in the civil service.[22] Jacques Chirac, an Enarch and member of the Cour des comptes, thus saw himself replaced by Gaullist barons of long-standing political experience,[23] whose mission was to drum up support for the presidential majority among the UDR rank and file, many of whom felt alienated from the new ministers in control of the successfully unified government.

Giscardization of the majority went hand in hand with an assumption of power by Independent Republican civil servants and industrialists,[24] who replaced the traditional notables; the elimination of the UDR from the executive was accomplished by replacing Gaullist bureaucrats with political operatives experienced in handling the local affairs that take on such decisive importance in legislative elections. If the Giscardians had taken over the executive, they nevertheless could not hope by themselves to win the impending legislative elections: they therefore needed UDR support to win a majority of the popular vote, the votes of the middle classes and the PME, of all those who felt threatened by the policy of all-out concentration and free competition favored by the Giscardians—allies of modern capitalism—and who could be tempted to abandon the UDR government in favor of a Giscardian one.

It is therefore impossible to agree with Georges Marchais* in his statement, made after the formation of the Barre government, that "there are no differences between the various factions that make up the Giscardian coalition, either in the policies to be carried out in behalf of capitalist big business or in the basic means to be used in achieving those ends."[25] On the contrary, the present coalition brings together men of very different socioprofessional backgrounds acting as spokesmen for social and economic interests that are often in radical conflict with one another. By refusing to waver from its "state monopoly capitalism" line, the Communist party minimizes the conflicts within the French bourgeoisie, and in some respects clings to the same attitude it adopted

---

*Leader of the PCF.—Trans.

in 1961 when faced with the Casanova-Servin analysis of Gaullism. In this regard, the reversal in the balance of power that has occurred since 1961 must be mentioned. At that time Gaullism represented modernizing capitalism and Antoine Pinay stood for the provincial bourgeoisie, the PME, today, the UDR siphons off the votes of the bedrock middle class, while the Independent Republicans stand for modern capitalism, though oriented more toward the Anglo-Saxon model and hostile to the state capitalism promoted under de Gaulle. This reversal in the positions of the partners in the majority is worthy of note in spite of the differences between the present situation and that of 1961.

To continue to deny, as in 1961, that the contradictions within the majority, typical of structural conflicts between hostile socioeconomic groups, have major importance, on the pretext that the basic contradiction is between the bourgeoisie as a whole and the working class, is to underestimate the fragility of the present governing coalition. It is also to fail to appreciate the attitude of UDR deputies like Hector Rolland, who has said that he wants to "form a grass-roots coalition of all who are dissatisfied, who have lost confidence in the people who govern us," and who has heaped scorn on the "technocrats" responsible for carrying out Giscard's policies.[26]

Giscardian modernism—which now has the support of the civil service and the assistance of big business and is not too proud to travel in the company of propagandists of American-style growth, like the journalists at *L'Express*—nevertheless still needs the old campaigners of the UDR, who know the art of politics and appreciate the value of ambiguity in holding on to electoral gains. The function of the UDR is no longer to govern, but rather to hold on to the support of social strata whose interests are steamrollered by Giscardian policies. These policies encourage the concentration of large firms, allow American capital to take over major companies, and profess a certain liberalism on moral issues (lowering of the age of majority, legalization of abortion, etc.), all actions that cannot but cause dismay in the provinces so dear to Georges Pompidou, Jacques Chirac, and Pierre Juillet. Giscardian policy—increasingly the target of attacks by the latter two men because it has often, as in the case of the capital gains law, been directed solely against the middle classes which have traditionally supported the Gaullist majority[27] —will from now on be prosecuted unswervingly.*

For this patchwork coalition to remain in power, the UDR must continue to play its role as a "catchall" party willing to support Giscardism in parliament, while the Giscardians in control of the government move with growing confidence to politicize the civil service and particularly the prefectoral corps.[28] In this realm Giscard's liberal society has received the backing of Jacques Chaban-Delmas, who is still pushing his plans for a "new society": capitalism, in this vision, is supposed to get the "stalled society" moving again, while the UDR battalions fight its parliamentary battles. The change in role inevitably entails changes in personnel.

The role assigned the UDR, made clear in the choice of Gaullists appointed to the government, is similar, moreover, to the role assigned Giscardism's other allies, which are also represented in the government by professional politicians outside the Giscardian contingent. The only new appointee to the Barre government not yet mentioned, Pierre Brousse, brought with him his experience as a Radical-Socialist mayor, a traditional notable adept at representing the interests of provincial France. Doubtless it was not by chance that he was named to head the Ministère du Commerce et de l'Artisanat, whose influence in swaying elections is no secret. The policy in effect since the adoption of the Royer Law has not been changed: the imperative is to hold on to the votes of small businessmen threatened by modernization of the retail sector, which once Valéry Giscard d'Estaing himself hoped to avoid slowing down any more than necessary.

The role of the UDR, like that of the Radicals and the CDS, is to "snare" the votes of Frenchmen attached to their past, their traditions, their small shops, and their stable existence, who have sometimes loudly expressed their fears not only of pursuing all-out modernization but also of its social and cultural consequences. The politicians representing these parties must therefore sink roots into the soil of conservative France

*Thus contributing to Giscard's defeat in the 1981 presidential elections.—Trans.

and at the same time try to hang on to the support that a portion of the working class has traditionally given to Gaullism. Only they can enable Giscardism, already represented in the government and before long to be represented in parliament as well by men of quite another sort, to carry out its own policies, designed to encourage modern capitalism. Hence this paradoxical coalition is quite tenuous.*

The attempt to recruit a new type of politician has not, however, escaped the notice of the majority's supporters, who have accepted it only with reluctance. Allied though they are with the RI against the forces of the left, Gaullist voters nonetheless find it hard to support new leaders preaching economic policies so detrimental to their own interests. With its desire to eliminate the distance between ministers and deputies, Giscardism has helped to lay bare the ambiguities that have until now permitted the Gaullist deputies to win the support of both the PME and a large segment of the working class.

Things being as they are, there is a good chance that the Giscardians will lose their bet, which is that they can keep the influence of the Gaullists in parliament in check while at the same time controlling the machinery of government under a regime in which the three major power centers are closely unified. The 1976 legislative by-elections made clear how unrealistic this program is, for the "real" France gave its support mainly to the Gaullist candidates or else to men such as Jean Royer, who stood up as spokesmen for a right wing with muscle, willing to defend the interests of a petty bourgeoisie threatened both by the giant firms that were coming more and more to stand for modern capitalism and by fresh efforts to liberalize the mores of the society. In this respect the new Gaullist coalition forming around Jacques Chirac may be seen as an attempt to resurrect the RPF. This accounts for the increasingly serious tensions between Giscardians and Gaullists: the Giscardians may win control of the executive, but they cannot hope to capture votes that still only the Gaullists know how to garner. The impossibility of a Gis-

---

*As Jacques Chirac's refusal to give unequivocal support to Giscard in the second round of the 1981 presidential elections makes clear.—Trans.

cardian victory in the legislative elections, then, means that Giscardism must still rely on the support of politicians who know how to get the attention of provincial France.

Conclusion

With this quick overview of the recent history of the French political system, we have seen how great a light can be shed on the nature of the state itself by analysis of the occupants of its top positions in each historical period. Indeed, the idea of the state is translated into reality in the form of specific institutions controlled by various groups within the ruling class, which often have close relations with certain social groups or classes whose interests are a long way from coinciding. As a result, conflicts within the social system inevitably have immediate repercussions on the machinery of government.

In certain periods of French history, one social class has succeeded in obtaining such tight control over society as a whole that it is able to dominate the government from within, running the governmental machinery through agents drawn from its midst. Such was the case during the July Monarchy: in such periods, the state would seem to have scarcely any distinctive character of its own. In France, however, this period of almost completely unified authority gave way, under the Third and Fourth Republics, to a period in which political, administrative, and economic powers were in distinctly separate hands. This came about because of the advent of a new group of professional politicians, sprung from the middle classes and the liberal professions and brought to the fore by large political parties that fought one another for the popular vote. If these professionals little by little gained control of both the legislature and the executive, they remained estranged from both business and the bureaucracy, whose power they did not find it easy to master. Riven by profound contradictions, the state harbored within it quite different sorts of personnel, who often came into conflict with one another. If, then, the state was no longer the mere instrument of an economically dominant class and was no longer run, as at one time it had been, by representatives of that class, still its autonomy remained quite tenuous, in that the professional politicians who were its leaders could not rely on the unstinting support of the bureaucrats specialized in the operation of the machinery of government.

Conversely, once it appeared that the institutionalization of the governmental structure was complete, and the governmental machinery had developed into a homogeneous, specialized bureaucracy whose ranks were filled in accordance with strictly meritocratic criteria, the idea became current that the state could aspire to independence and sever itself entirely from the social system. Insofar as it could rely on its own resources (the army, the bureaucracy), it was thought that the state could assume responsibility for the entire society. From Bonapartism to Gaullism, this claim to independence on the part of the state has been a recurring feature of French political history.

Under the Fifth Republic, for example, senior civil servants took control of the executive and abandoned parliament to the professional politicians, who thereafter tended to express not national but local interests, while the executive took charge of the regulation of the social system. The partial unification of the executive and the bureaucracy, and the estrangement, due to the recruitment methods used, of this newly unified leadership group from both the business world and the professional politicians who represented conflicting special interests, gave rise once again to a claim to independence on the part of the state. The government tried to make good this claim by instituting, for example, an activist and more or less centrally planned economic policy designed to make use of bureaucratic expertise to tighten the state's grip on the social system.

However much they may have wished it, the bureaucrats wedded to the concept of an independent state could not remain indefinitely "suspended in the air," cut off from society's grass roots. The interventionist economic policy they pursued in the name of the state led willy-nilly to a strengthening of the power of special interests, whose collaboration became indispensable. By claiming independence, then, the state legitimized its more or less authoritarian intervention, which in the end worked in favor of the dominant economic forces.

Once the governmental machine had accomplished its mission of modernization, the state no longer tried to maintain its independence. While the bureaucracy has clung to its distinctive role by recruiting from within and shutting out representatives of, say, the business world, its leaders have by all appearances moved to tighten their ties with business. The trend has been toward a new and broader unification of politico-administrative and economic powers: Gaullism, in other words, has given way to Giscardism. But by revealing too much of its true nature, this new unity may well become more and more tenuous as time goes by, for it will no longer be able to claim the legitimacy afforded the state by the fact that it aspires to be independent.

Postscript, 1981

Victory in the June 1981 legislative elections gave the Socialist party and its allies control of the French parliament. Having previously won the presidency,* the Socialists, long powerful at the local level, have carried off a sweeping conquest of *electoral* power in France. However, the French political system, as we have seen, is one in which the state is governed by certain principles. It is highly autonomous within a public sphere distinct from the private sphere, and it is run by a highly organized civil service, which adheres to the notion that its actions are governed by an idea of the public interest and which attempts to shield the administration from the influence of groups within the society presumed to be special-interest groups. Hence the Socialist victory via universal suffrage is not equivalent to a conquest of the *state*.

It is evident that such a paradoxical situation can only occur in countries whose political structure, the result of specific historical circumstances, affords such a unique position to the state. The burden of history continues to make itself felt even today. As a result, there seems to be, in France today and perhaps in Spain tomorrow, a contradiction between "statist" and "parliamentarist" principles of legitimacy. By contrast, in countries like Great Britain, where the growth of statism was limited by quick acceptance of parliamentarist principles, a Labor party victory at the polls means that the Labor party will soon control, to all intents and purposes, the central government. Even if the Labor government runs up against hostility from the civil service, that alone is really no obstacle to the exercise of power, because the power of the civil service is tenuous. If Labor governments have generally been moder-

---

*With François Mitterrand's victory over Valéry Giscard d'Estaing on May 10, 1981.—Trans.

ate in their objectives, the reason for their caution is not to be found in the existence of a strong state apparatus hostile to the government's intentions.

In France, however, the state has always gained its power at the expense of *parlement*,* and the very idea of representative government was slow to take hold and was finally accepted only in difficult circumstances. The universalism of the state was based on the universalism of the citizen, considered in the abstract, independent of any partisan allegiance. With legitimacy supported by the twin pillars of state and citizen, the representation of special interests could not help but be seen as almost illegitimate. This explains why the party system in France is so weak and why there are virtually no strong pressure groups and lobbyist organizations of the sort that play such an important role in the Anglo-Saxon democracies. In France the administration prefers to elaborate national policy by itself, without interference from either elected representatives or interest groups. Taking upon itself the task of spokesman for the general interest, the administration believes that it can guarantee the independence of the state.

It can be argued that, over the course of history, the particular character of the French state has been subjected to two radically different kinds of threats. In certain periods the ruling class has wanted to assume direct political power by reducing the state structure to a minimum: under the July Monarchy, for example, the ruling class impaired the state to such a degree that it lost all legitimacy. Social conflict was exacerbated as a result, eventually leading to a revolution that brought about a return to a strong and independent state. At other times the state has been threatened by democracy: statist principles of legitimacy were again in trouble under the Third and Fourth Republics. Once again the result was social and political instability, leading to the revival of a strong state. Ultimately, the Fifth Republic ushered in a period in which parliament was dominated by the government, the power of the ruling class was reduced, and the state apparatus claimed supremacy. With the advent of Giscard d'Estaing, however, the character of certain state institutions, as they had developed since De Gaulle, was once again called into question:

*In both the old and the new senses.—Trans.

professing to believe in "liberalism," Giscard steamrollered those institutions that got in his way and at the same time increased the power of the ruling class. Traditionally, then, whenever state institutions have been called into question by one regime or another, a return to statist principles of legitimation has always ensued. Today, however, following the Giscardian episode, there is reason to believe that such a return may not occur. For reasons quite different from those of Giscard, the new Socialist majority may also work against the unity of government and administration implicit in the statist system.

It is worth stressing, however, that the Constitution of the Fifth Republic, inherently statist in its mode of legitimation, remains unchanged in spite of the change of majority. Returned to power after an extended hiatus, the left has not tampered with the semipresidential regime instituted by the 1958 Constitution. It has taken no steps to reinstate the parliamentary regime that had brought it to power under the Third and Fourth Republics. The reason is simple: for the first time the left is now the beneficiary of the constitutional provisions adopted by its adversaries and once combatted by its supporters. Today as before, the president of the Republic has powers more extensive than those of the president of the United States or the prime minister of Great Britain. Time is on his side, moreover. Socialism's "tranquil force"* now exerts itself through the institutions of the Gaullist state. "I am accommodating to the institutions," President Mitterrand has stated.[1]

So the supremacy of the presidency has been left intact and few changes have been made in the legislature. Increasing the power of the legislature is not among the first priorities of the present government. There has been no diminution in the power to govern by executive order and no augmentation in the power of the legislature to legislate. There have been no changes in the procedure by which the legislative agenda is set, and there has been no increase in the power of legislative committees, which play such an important role in the parliamentary democracies. In practice, moreover, the Socialist

---

*Mitterrand's slogan in the presidential election campaign was that he represented *la force tranquille*—Trans.

party is tightly controlled by emissaries from the executive branch, so that in effect the government commands an automatic majority in parliament. Certain recent votes, such as the vote on energy policy, show clearly that the parliamentary party is subordinate to the government. When a delegate to the Socialist Party Congress declared that the party was not merely the government's "hobnailed boot," Jean-Pierre Chevènement, currently minister of technology and research, responded that the hobnailed boot was "a good, comfortable sort of shoe."[2]

Thus the regime remains essentially semipresidential and statist. Nevertheless, its unity has been impaired by certain important changes. The Socialist victory has brought back the "Republic of Schoolteachers" and put an end to the "Republic of Functionaries," which was already on the way out under Giscard. Even more clearly, the Socialist victory has destroyed the expanded integration of authority that had developed in recent years. One deputy in three is presently a teacher. Fifty-eight percent of the deputies belonging to the Socialist party or to the center-left Mouvement des Radicaux de Gauche (M.R.G.) are teachers. Of 108 deputies who teach in secondary schools, 94 belong to the P.S. or M.R.G. Even though the Socialist party now occupies the heights of power, it has not always given key posts to senior civil servants at the expense of the schoolteachers in its ranks. The percentage of schoolteachers in the parliamentary contingent has gone from 40 to 58 percent, whereas the percentage of senior civil servants has risen from 12 to 22 percent. Of the forty-one Communist deputies, not one is a senior civil servant.

The head of the government is a former secondary school teacher who long served as a union militant as well; nearly 30 percent of the members of the government also once worked as secondary school teachers. By contrast, the percentage of technocratic intellectuals (senior civil servants and professors of law, economics, medicine, etc.) has been cut in half (from 56 percent in the Barre government to 28 percent in the present [Mauroy] government). Only 14 percent of the Mauroy government are Enarchs, compared with as many as 30 percent under certain previous governments. The composition of the ministerial staffs has also changed considerably. Seventy-five percent of staff aides under the last Barre government were senior civil servants. The comparable figure under the Mauroy government is only 54 percent. By contrast, the percentage of school teachers on ministerial staffs has risen from 4.4 to 9.5 percent. Even more noteworthy is the increase in the number of party employees and officials of unions and other organizations serving on ministerial staffs: from 0.2 to 10.2 percent. Whereas there were 226 Enarchs working for the Barre government, there are only 152 working for Mauroy's ministers.[3]

Thus in many respects the Socialist Fifth Republic seems comparable to governments under the Third and Fourth Republic: the importance of teachers, the relative eclipse of the senior civil service, and the return of the professional politicians. It is worth noting, however, that workers are missing from this predominantly left-wing Assembly: 6 of the 285 Socialist deputies are workers, as are 15 of the 44 Communist deputies. Note, too, that the doctors, lawyers, and journalists so prominent under the two republics in which the democratic principle held sway have almost entirely vanished. This leads to the hypothesis that national politicians will be less swayed by local issues than they were under the Third and Fourth Republics, since school teachers are not generally local notables to the same degree as doctors, lawyers, and pharmacists. This may impede the reconstitution of old clientele networks, even in cases where the newly elected deputy already enjoys a certain local power-base as a result of having been elected to a municipal or general council.

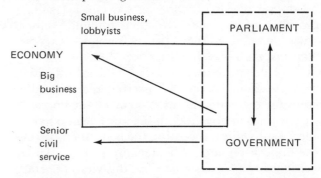

Figure 1. Tendencies of the Socialist Fifth Republic

Composed mainly of secondary school teachers, the Socialist majority has shown a propensity to favor universalistic, moralistic views of the world, sometimes compatible with rather rudimentary versions of Marxism. Even when the Socialist party was still in opposition, it never really achieved a coherent theory of society and often used terminology borrowed from the Communists in its party platforms and training sessions. This explains why, as an opposition party, the Socialists waged a campaign against the "fat cats," and why they were willing to make do with the deficiencies in the theory of the state underlying such a campaign.[4] It further explains why the Socialist party was so attracted to the theory of "state monopoly capitalism" despite the obvious defects of such a theory as applied to the French case, where the state is so highly differentiated from civil society.

For the French Communist party, the state is of course the "instrument" whereby the class that owns the means of production maintains and reproduces its domination. The nature, organization, and structure of the state are essentially determined by its "class content."[5] The Socialist party has also subscribed at times to an equally reductionist theory of the state, maintaining that the state was controlled by "monopoly capital" or by the "financial oligarchy."[6] If the left-wing parties really believe these arguments, logic should compel them to destroy the state in order to put socialist policies into practice. In so doing the Socialist party would be harking back, bizarrely, to Jules Guesde's notion that "the government... and the capitalists are one" and to Guesde's battle cry, "Hit the State!"[7] In other words, the Socialists would be making their own the ideas of the enemy of their founding father, Jean Jaurès, who maintained that "the state is not bourgeois, and to say that it is, is an oversimplification."[8]

In the televised debate between Valéry Giscard d'Estaing and François Mitterrand, Mitterrand asserted that "it is the right that builds up the state, not us. You made the bureaucracy. You are the ones in power."[9] In the same vein, one key Socialist leader, Paul Quilès, recently attacked "the obstructionism of the opposition and its lieutenants, some of whom hold high positions in the civil service." In this view, the state is controlled by the conservative opposition and is being used to protect business interests. During the debate on nationalization of certain industries and banks, one Socialist deputy spoke of "family ties between some politicians in yesterday's majority and the big bank-holding companies."[10] Apparently, some Socialists do not accept the argument that the state is institutionalized and distinct from civil society. This naturally tempts them to resort to a "spoils sytem" of a sort usually associated with countries in which the state is not really institutionalized, such as the United States.

What we seem to be witnessing, then, is a challenge to statist principles of legitimation. Now, throughout French history, statist principles have been associated with the so-called Grandes Ecoles, and in recent years particularly with the Ecole Nationale d'Administration (ENA). The Socialist party platform emphasized the need for "a rapid democratization of the senior civil service, by changing methods of recruitment and promotion and adopting a new salary structure." By the same token, the Communist civil service minister Anicet Le Pors has said that the ENA must be changed in order to open up the administrative apparatus in such a way as "to reflect French society" by taking in "local elected officials, union officials, and leaders of cooperative groups."[11] Moreover, there is reason to think that the new law concerning decentralization will also raise challenges to statist principles of legitimation. Under this law, the prefects, long the champions of the general interest on which the statist principle rests, are to be replaced by Commissaires de la République, and some of the powers that once belonged to the prefect are to be transferred to the presidents* of the *départemental* general council and regional council.[12] Add to that the proposal to allow Corsica to elect a local assembly by universal suffrage, a change that will also work against the unity of the state.

The attitude of many Socialists toward the state and the senior civil service is a sign that there is once again, as under the Third and Fourth Republics, a gulf between some politicians and some top civil servants. Even the organization of the senior civil service into Grands Corps has been questioned. Even though the left now enjoys extensive constitutional

*Elected officials.—Trans.

powers, it seems somewhat cut off from other crucial sources of power in the top levels of the administration and, even more, in the business world.

Thus we have the apparent paradox of a political force that is extraordinarily powerful and yet still fragile. Its extraordinary power comes from the fact that the Socialist government is the first under the Fifth Republic to enjoy control of both the executive and legislative branches and a majority of the municipal governments (since the 1977 municipal elections) together with support from the big unions, which seem ready to restrain the restive rank-and-file, as well as substantial support from the media (television, radio, newspapers). The Socialist government is in the process of considerably expanding the public sector by nationalizing a number of large banks and industries. It also has the support of a fair number of local associations. Assured, moreover, of disciplined backing by the left-wing parties, the government is extending its influence over the whole of society. But the new regime seems bent on ignoring what is peculiar about the history of the state in France and determined to replace the institutionalized state by a centralized power controlled by a political party or coalition, a power which is compatible with a certain form of controlled decentralization. Accordingly, the program of the new regime would seem to follow a logic at odds with the inherent logic of the state.

Notes

Chapter 1

1. Pierre Legendre, *Histoire de l'administration de 1750 à nos jours* (Paris: Presses Universitaires de France, 1968), p. 545.
2. Karl Marx, *The Eighteenth Brumaire of Louis Bonaparte* (New York: International Publishers, 1963), p. 62.
3. Ibid., p. 67.
4. Ibid., p. 118.
5. Ibid., p. 121.
6. Ibid., p. 131.
7. Ibid., p. 122.
8. Nicos Poulantzas, *Pouvoir politique et Classes sociales* (Paris: Maspero, 1968), p. 145 (trans. as *Political Power and Social Classes* [London: New Left Books, 1975]).
9. Marx, *The Eighteenth Brumaire*, p. 61. For a recent study of the uses of the Bonapartist model in the Marxist literature, see Alain Rouquié, "L'hypothèse 'bonapartiste' et l'émergence des systèmes politiques semi-compétitifs," *Revue française de science politique* (December 1975).
10. Marx, *The Eighteenth Brumaire*, p. 121.
11. Louis Girard, *La Politique des travaux publics sous le Second Empire* (Paris: Armand Colins, 1952).
12. Karl Marx, *The Civil War in France* (New York: International Publishers, 1940), p. 56.
13. Poulantzas, *Pouvoir politique*, pp. 308-12.
14. Karl Marx, *Critique of Hegel's "Philosophy of Right,"* trans. Annette Jolin and Joseph O'Malley (Cambridge, England: Cambridge University Press, 1970, corrected 1972), p. 45.
15. Ibid., p. 46. See Pierre Birnbaum, *Le Pouvoir politique* (Paris: Dalloz, 1975), pp. 8-9.
16. Vincent Wright, *Le Conseil d'Etat sous le second Empire* (Paris: Armand Colin, 1972), p. 57.
17. Bernard Le Clerc and Vincent Wright, *Les Préfets du second Empire* (Paris: Armand Colin, 1973), p. 181.

18. Vincent Wright, "Les directeurs et secrétaires généraux des administrations centrales sous le second Empire," in *Les Directeurs des ministères en France (XIX-XXe siècle)* (Geneva: Droz, 1976), p. 44.

19. William Serman, "Les généraux francais de 1870," *Revue de défense nationale* (August-September 1970):1330.

20. Le Clerc and Wright, *Les Préfets*, p. 160.

21. See the comparative table given by Wright in "Les directeurs," p. 46.

22. Cited by Wright, *Le Conseil d'Etat*, p. 174.

23. See Vincent Wright, "L'Ecole nationale d'administration de 1848-1849: un échec révélateur," *Revue historique* (January 1976).

24. See Theodore Zeldin, *The Political System of Napoleon III* (New York: Norton, 1971), pp. 10 and 52.

25. Henri Claude, *Gaullisme et Grand Capital* (Paris: Editions sociales, n.d.), p. 211.

26. Henri Claude, *Pouvoir économique et Pouvoir gaulliste* (Paris: Editions sociales, n.d.), p. 270.

27. Charles de Gaulle, *Mémoires de guerre* (Paris: Plon, 1959), p. 277.

28. "Marcel Servin répond à vos questions," *France nouvelle* (June 28, 1960):9.

29. Michel Hincker, "La bourgeoisie en quête de son pouvoir," *Economie et Politique* (March 1960):11 and 13.

30. Guy Landrelle, "Les dessous de l'affaire Pinay," *France nouvelle* (January 14, 1960):12.

31. Serge Mallet, *Le Gaullisme et la Gauche* (Paris: Editions du Seuil, 1965), p. 105.

32. Maurice Thorez, *France nouvelle* (February 1, 1961), p. 16.

33. See Jean Poperen, *La Gauche française* (Paris: Fayard, 1972), chap. 12; and Philippe Robrieux, *Maurice Thorez* (Paris: Fayard, 1975), chap. 9.

34. For instance, Serge Mallet contended that "the high administration, substantially reconstituted as a result of the new functions that have been assigned to it, has been tapped... to play the role of an arbitrator." See *Le Gaullisme et la Gauche*, p. 116.

35. The comparison with Napoleon III has been made by authors holding diverse views: for example, Brohm, Touvais, Pellegrini, and Frank have shown that "the state, as the agent and errand-boy of the bourgeoisie, has increasingly been playing the role of its own representative," because de Gaulle, "in the Fifth Republic had played the part of the 'Bonaparte' of capitalist France," in *Le Gaullisme et après?* (Paris: Maspero, 1974), pp. 22 and 215. From an opposite point of view, Philippe Herzog, after setting forth the theory of the CME, offers the judgment that "governmental institutions and bureaucracies have no history of their own, i.e., no history independent of, or even external

to, the history of the mode of production," in *Politique économique et Planification en régime capitaliste* (Paris: Editions sociales, 1972), p. 67.

Chapter 2

1. See Jean Lhomme's study of the law of the three powers in *La Grande Bourgeoisie au pouvoir: 1830-1880* (Paris, 1960).
2. André-Jean Tudesq, *Les Grands Notables en France, 1840-1849* (Paris: Presses Universitaires de France, 1964), 1:366.
3. See René Rémond, *La Droite en France* (Paris: Aubier, 1963), p. 88.
4. Guillaume de Bertier de Sauvigny, *La Restauration* (Paris: Flammarion, 1955), stresses the importance of functionaries in Restoration politics.
5. François Julien-Laferrière, *Les Députés-Fonctionnaires sous la monarchie de Juillet* (Paris: Presses Universitaires de France, 1970), pp. 44-54 and 94-100.
6. Ibid., chap. 2.
7. Ibid., pp. 99-100.
8. André-Jean Tudesq, *La France des notables* (Editions du Seuil, 1973), 1:143.
9. Tudesq, *Les Grands Notables*, 1:381.
10. Ibid., p. 339.
11. André-Jean Tudesq, *Les Conseillers généraux en France au temps de Guizot* (Paris: Armand Colin, 1967), p. 144.
12. The Second Empire has already been treated in the first chapter, and we shall not examine it again here. Our previous analysis allowed us to elaborate a model that makes sense of the state's claim to independence, a model that we shall be looking at in relation to other historical situations in order to discover the unique features of each.
13. See Georges Lavau, "La dissociation des pouvoirs," *Esprit* (June 1953):824.
14. Daniel Halévy, *La République des ducs* (Paris: Grasset, 1937), pp. 354-55.
15. Cited by Pierre Barral, *Les Fondateurs de la IIIe République* (Paris: Armand Colin, 1968), p. 230.
16. Speech of June 1, 1874, cited in ibid., p. 232.
17. Robert de Jouvenel, *La République des camarades* (Paris: Grasset, 1924), p. 37.
18. Jacques Kayser, *Les Grandes Batailles du radicalisme, 1820-1901* (Paris: M. Rivière, 1962), p. 291.
19. André Tardieu, *La Profession parlementaire* (Paris: Flammarion, 1937), p. 103.
20. Albert Thibaudet, *La République des professeurs* (Paris, Grasset,

1927), p. 158. See Georges Dupuis, "Albert Thibaudet," *Centenaire de la IIIe République* (Paris: Editions universitaires, 1975), p. 271.

21. Max Weber, "Politics as a Vocation," in H. H. Gerth and C. Wright Mills, eds., *From Max Weber: Essays in Sociology* (New York: Oxford University Press, 1946), p. 83.

22. Ibid., p. 86.

23. Gaetano Mosca, *The Ruling Class* (New York: McGraw-Hill, 1939), p. 258.

24. Ibid., p. 389.

25. Joseph Schumpeter, *Capitalism, Socialism, and Democracy* (New York: Harper and Row, 1942), p. 285.

26. Yves Henri Gaudemet, *Les Juristes et la Vie politique de la IIIe République* (Paris: Presses Universitaires de France, 1970), p. 74. Concerning lawyers, doctors, and teachers under the Third Republic, see Theodore Zeldin, *France, 1848-1945* (Oxford: The Clarendon Press, 1973), chap. 19. See also Guy Rossi-Landi, *Les Hommes politiques* (Paris: Presses Universitaires de France, 1973), pp. 22 ff.

27. Matei Dogan, "La stabilité du personnel parlementaire sous la IIIe République," *Revue française de science politique* (April-June 1953):335.

28. Matei Dogan, "Political Ascent in a Class Society: French Deputies 1870-1958," in Dwaine Marvick, ed., *Political Decision-Makers* (New York: The Free Press, 1961), p. 79.

29. André Siegfried, *De la IVe à la Ve* (Paris: Grasset, 1958), p. 64.

30. See, for example, Pierre Barral, *Le Département de l'Isère sous la IIIe République* (Paris: Armand Colin, 1962), pp. 326-27. In Isère the "new strata" did not emerge until 1895.

31. On Edouard Herriot, see Francis de Tarr, *The French Radical Party* (London: Oxford University Press, 1961), chap. 3.

32. This comparison is defective, however, in that the two tables do not report figures for exactly the same period. Unfortunately no other data are available.

33. See Jean Bouvier, "Aux origines de la IIIe République? Les réflexes sociaux des milieux d'affaires," *Revue historique* (October-December 1953); Guy Palmade, *Capitalisme et Capitalistes français au XIXe siècle* (Paris: Armand Colin, 1961), pp. 208-16; Jean-Noël Jeanneney, *François de Wendel en République* (Paris: Editions du Seuil, 1975), p. 233.

34. Halévy, *La République des ducs*, pp. 311 and 316.

35. Madeleine Reberioux, *La République radicale? 1898-1914* (Paris: Editions du Seuil, 1975), p. 233.

36. Ibid., p. 224. Similarly, Jean-Pierre Azema and Michel Winock contend that "by making some formal concessions, [the bourgeoisie]

was able to place the state at its service," in *La IIIe République* (Paris: Calmann-Levy, 1969, reissued 1976), p. 117.

37. Poulantzas, *Pouvoir politique*, p. 272.

38. Ibid., p. 334.

39. Gambetta, speech of September 18, 1878, in Pierre Barral, *Les Fondateurs*, p. 318.

40. Vincent Wright, "L'épuration du Conseil d'Etat, juillet 1879," *Revue d'histoire moderne et contemporaine* (October–December 1972): 643.

41. Concerning the origins of the Ecole libre des sciences politiques, see Pierre Rain, *L'Ecole libre des sciences politiques* (Paris: Fondation nationale des sciences politiques, 1963). Concerning the Conseil d'Etat, see Marie-Christine Kessler, *Le Conseil d'Etat* (Paris: Armand Colin, 1968), p. 150. For a more general treatment, see also Jean-Marie Mayeur, *Les Débuts de la IIIe République* (Paris: Editions du Seuil, 1973), p. 87.

42. See Jeanne Siwek-Pouydesseau, *Le Corps préfectoral sous la IIIe et la IVe République* (Paris: Armand Colin, 1969), pp. 77-79.

43. François Bédarida, "L'armée et la République: les opinions politiques des officiers français en 1876-1878," *Revue historique* (September 1964).

44. Raoul Girardet, *La Société militaire dans la France contemporaine* (Paris: Plon, 1963), p. 198.

45. Robert de Jouvenel, *La République des camarades*, pp. 98 ff.

46. Though the contrast was not always pronounced, the different tasks assigned to each of these two groups are worthy of note. In particular, the role of the cabinets in accelerating French industrialization during the Third Republic should be given prominence. See Pierre Legendre, "Les cabinets ministériels de la IIIe République," *Origine et Histoire des cabinets des ministres en France* (Geneva: Droz, 1975), p. 77.

Chapter 3

1. For example, the sharp decline of senior civil servants among the conseillers généraux should be noted. There were 248 of them out of a total group of 2,798 in 1870 (see Louis Girard, André Prost, and Robert Gossez, *Les Conseillers généraux en 1870* [Paris: PUF, 1967], p. 47) and 66 out of a total of 5,367 under the Fourth Republic (see Marie-Hélène Marchand, *Les Conseillers généraux en France depuis 1945* [Paris: Armand Colin, 1970], p. 59). Similarly, as we noted earlier, there were many members of the Conseil d'Etat among the conseillers généraux of the July Monarchy (see André-Jean Tudesq, *Les Conseillers généraux en France du temps de Guizot*, p. 139). Practically none remained in the Fourth Republic.

2. Matei Dogan, "Les filières de la carrière politique en France," p. 481. See Jean Charlot, "Les élites politiques en France de la IIIe à la Ve République," *Archives européennes de sociologie* 14 (1973).

3. Matei Dogan, "Political Ascent in a Class Society," p. 79.

4. Matei Dogan and Peter Campbell, "Le personnel ministériel en France et en Grande-Bretagne, 1945-1957," *Revue française de science politique* (April-June 1957):323.

5. In all, 231 deputies in this legislature were not reelected. We have not counted the Communists, for whom the problem is completely different. Our sample involved 87 persons for whom we could find career records. The main source used was *Who's Who?* This work was carried out with the help of Bertrand Badie, an assistant in the Political Science Department at the University of Paris I.

6. We have looked only at ministers, and not at secretaries of state or subsecretaries. Of the 146 former ministers, 17 died shortly after leaving office. For information sources we used *Who's Who?*, the *Annuaire Chateaudun*, and questionnaires sent to all the ministers.

7. The characteristics were defined as follows:

Regression: this category included (1) ex-members of parliament who, after leaving office, did not find a position equivalent or superior to the one they had held before their first election, and (2) ex-members of parliament who, after leaving office, were unable to reverse the slowing of their professional activities that had occurred while they held their posts.

Stagnation: included under this head were ex-MP's whose professional situation neither improved nor deteriorated as a result of their stint in parliament.

Retirement: includes all ex-MP's who ceased—or did not resume—their professional activities after leaving office.

Improvement of professional status: includes ex-MP's who continued to practice their original profession and were able to improve their status therein during or after their time in office (in such ways as an upgrading or expansion of clientele, a "move up" to Paris, etc.).

Change of profession: includes ex-MP's who changed profession after leaving office to a new position of higher status.

Career in politics: includes ex-MP's who did not return to their original occupation after leaving office, choosing instead to make politics their full-time occupation (as mayors of large cities, party officials, editors of political newspapers, etc.).

8. This remark is particularly apt for the RPF, which is made up chiefly of senior bureaucrats, officers, and corporate directors.

9. Of the ministers in the sample, 4.5 percent were considered unclassifiable.

10. If we look at the professional development of ministers in the

same way as we have done for members of parliament, we find that only 9 percent of former ministers improved their professional status or switched to a new profession of higher status. Few former ministers, then, profited professionally by their service in the government. Things would be quite different under the Fifth Republic.

11. André Siegfried, *De la IVe à la Ve*, p. 220.

12. Pierre Lalumière, *L'Inspection des Finances* (Paris: Presses Universitaires de France, 1959), pp. 38–39.

13. Georges Lavau, *Partis politiques et Classes sociales* (Paris: Armand Colin, 1955), p. 117.

14. Rather curiously, it is apparently impossible to find complete and accurate statistics regarding the socioprofessional background of members of the Grands Corps under the Fourth Republic. The only data available have to do with the socioprofessional background of ENA students: see Thomas Bottomore, "La mobilité sociale dans la haute administration," *Cahiers internationaux de sociologie* 13(1952).

15. De Jouvenel, *La Republique des camarades*, pp. 98 ff.

16. Concerning the socioprofessional background of staff members under the Fourth Republic, see Jean-Louis Seurin, "Les cabinets ministériels," *Revue de droit public et de la science politique* (November-December 1956):1293–94.

17. Pierre Lalumière, *L'Inspection des Finances*, pp. 162–69.

18. Dessler, *Le Conseil d'Etat*, p. 236. Between 1946 and 1958, 160 members of the Conseil d'Etat served on ministerial staffs.

19. Pierrette Rongère, *La Cour des comptes* (Paris: Fondation nationale des sciences politiques, 1963).

20. Jeanne Siwek-Pouydesseau, *Le Corps préfectoral sous la IIIe et IVe Republique*, p. 149. The author shows that 49 percent of prefects in the Fourth Republic served on ministerial staffs.

21. These data are drawn from the thesis of G. Lafouge, which was presented to a graduate seminar I ran at the University of Paris I in 1976: "Les Cabinets des présidents du Conseil de la IVe République" (thesis, University of Paris I, 1976). The complete sample comprises 246 persons, not counting 19 unknowns and the various staff attaches.

22. See Seurin, "Les cabinets ministériels," p. 1293.

23. See Henry Ehrmann, *Organized Business in France*, (Princeton: Princeton University Press, 1957). See also Georges Lavau, "Note sur un 'pressure group' français: la CGPME," *Revue française de science politique* 5, no. 2 (1955).

24. Concerning doctors, see Jean Meynaud, *Les Groupes de pression en France* (Paris: Armand Colin, 1958), pp. 209 ff.

25. Ehrmann, *Organized Business*. See also Philip Williams, *French Politicians and Elections: 1951–1969* (Cambridge, England: Cambridge University Press, 1970), p. 226 ff.

Chapter 4

1. Nicholas Wahl, "Aux origines de la nouvelle Constitution," *Revue française de science politique* (May 1959):60 ff.
2. Roland Cayrol, Jean-Luc Parodi, and Colette Ysmal, *Le Député français* (Paris: Armand Colin, 1973), p. 43.
3. Ibid., p. 42. See Jean Charlot, "Les élites politiques en France de la IIIe à la IVe République," *Archives européennes de sociologie* 14 (1973).
4. Cayrol et al., *Le Député français*. The authors themselves recognize that "the social functions of doctors, their status as 'men with connections,' and their high standing in the community all make it likely they will gain access to parliament." In our view, however, doctors can hardly be classed among the "ruling groups."
5. Olgierd Lewandowski, "L'image sociale de l'élite d'après le *Who's Who in France?*" *Revue française de sociologie* (January–March 1974): 63.
6. Cayrol et al., *Le Député français*, p. 40.
7. Ibid.
8. Ibid., p. 66.
9. Ibid., pt. 2, chap. 2, where the authors themselves take account of other factors such as political traditions, and in particular the influence of religious traditions.
10. See Marchand, *Les Conseillers généraux*, p. 161.
11. Jean-Francois Médard, "La recherche du cumul des mandats par les candidats aux élections législatives sous la Ve République," *Les Facteurs locaux de la vie politique nationale* (Paris: Pedone, 1972), p. 141. In the same vein see also Cayrol et al., *Le Député français*, p. 115.
12. Pierre Birnbaum, "Les détenteurs du pouvoir politique local dans la France de la Ve République," in Jacques Lagroye and Vincent Wright, eds., *Local Power* (London: Allen and Unwin, 1977).
13. Ezra Suleiman, *Politics, Power, and Bureaucracy in France* (Princeton: Princeton University Press, 1974), chap. 6, shows how civil servants eschewed contact with deputies while claiming to defend the general interest against special interests.
14. See Philip Williams, *The French Parliament, 1958–1967* (London: Allen and Unwin, 1966), p. 115.
15. Jean-Pierre Worms, "Le préfet et ses notables," *Sociologie du travail* (July–September 1966).
16. See Jean-Claude Escarras et al., *Courrier parlementaire et Fonction parlementaire* (Paris: Presses Universitaires de France, 1971), pp. 28 and 79.
17. André Chandernagor, *Un Parlement pour quoi faire?* (Paris: Gallimard, 1967), p. 22.
18. These findings should, however, be used with caution: since

there were very few former RI ministers (six), we naturally did not consider the professional development of the ministers in the Chirac government under Giscard's presidency. Moreover, centrist ex-ministers generally went over to the opposition during the course of the Fifth Republic.

19. A greater professionalization of politics than in the Fourth Republic should be noted. In the Fifth, participation in the government signified the beginning of a career in politics for 6 percent of the ex-ministers. The comparable figure for the Fourth Republic was only 1.4 percent. The cause of this phenomenon lies with the presence of senior bureaucrats in the governments of the Fifth Republic.

Chapter 5

1. Pascal Antoni and Jean-Dominique Antoni, *Les Ministres de la Ve République* (Paris, 1976), p. 13.
2. Ibid., pp. 22 ff. Concerning the influence of senior bureaucrats in the Fifth Republic, see Charles Debbasch, *L'Administration au pouvoir* (Paris: Calmann-Levy, 1969), pp. 72 ff.
3. Jacques Chevalier, "L'intérêt général dans l'administration française," *Revue internationale des sciences administratives* 4 (1975), pp. 326-27.
4. Matei Dogan, "Comment on devient ministre en France, 1870-1976," *Proceedings of the International Association of Political Sciences Congress* (Edinburgh, August 1976), p. 16.
5. Antoni and Antoni, *Les Ministres de la Ve République*, p. 34.
6. Jeanne Siwek-Pouydesseau, *Le Personnel de direction des ministères* (Paris: Armand Colin, 1969), p. 46.
7. Siwek-Pouydesseau, *Le Corps préfectoral*, p. 149.
8. Kessler, *Le Conseil d'Etat*, p. 237. Concerning the Cour des comptes and participation by its members on ministerial staffs, see Rongère, *La Cour des comptes*, p. 105.
9. Alain Darbel and Dominique Schnapper, *Le Système administratif* (Paris: Mouton, 1972), p. 142.
10. Many students entering the ENA have fathers who are civil servants, but fathers in the senior ranks are less well represented. In 1972, for example, 20 students out of 63 had a father who was a senior civil servant, and 8 out of 32 in the internal competition. Source: *Archives de l'ENA*.
11. See Jeanne Siwek-Pouydesseau, "Les cabinets ministériels," *Les Superstructures des administrations centrales* (Paris: Cujas, 1973), p. 35.
12. Bertrand Badie and Pierre Birnbaum, "L'autonomie des institutions politico-administratives: le rôle des cabinets des présidents de la République et des Premiers ministres sous la Ve République," *Revue française de science politique* (April 1976):289.

13. Ibid., p. 296.

14. Ibid., pp. 296-300.

15. Special appointments to the Inspection des Finances were begun in 1974. Only three persons have been recruited in this way [as of November 1976—trans.], one in 1974, one in 1975, and a third in 1976. Unlike the Conseil d'Etat and the Cour des comptes, the Inspection des Finances has thus withstood political pressure and been more successful in maintaining its distinctive functional character, an impression which is only strengthened by the fact that none of the three individuals mentioned above seems to have served on a ministerial staff prior to being named to the Inspection.

16. This work was carried out in collaboration with Veronique Aubert.

17. Siwek-Pouydesseau, *Le Corps préfectoral*, p. 21.

18. Kessler, *Le Conseil d'Etat*, p. 163, has also noticed the large number of prefects named as special appointees to the Conseil d'Etat, but she does not regard these appointments as political. There is reason to contend, however, that these individuals have played genuinely political roles in their careers. In this connection, it would be very interesting to know specifically what projects were undertaken by former prefects on the Conseil d'Etat. Unfortunately, such information seems impossible to obtain, in view of the secrecy that shrouds the activities of the Conseil. Furthermore, Kessler does not consider the role played by the transitional service on a ministerial staff prior to nomination to the Conseil.

19. Siwek-Pouydesseau, *Le Personnel de direction*, pp. 84-88.

20. See, for example, Jeanne Siwek-Pouydesseau, "French Ministerial Staffs," in Matei Dogan, ed., *The Mandarins of Western Europe* (New York: John Wiley and Sons, 1975), pp. 198-99.

21. In November 1976, for example, Pierre Mazeaud was named by special appointment to the Conseil d'Etat a short while after leaving the post of secretary of state for youth and sports. As a result, he did not attempt to regain his seat as a deputy in the next by-election.

22. One of these two was Marie-France Garaud, whose particularly active role on Georges Pompidou's staff is well known; the other was Pierre Juillet. See chapter 7, on Giscardism.

23. Rongère, *La Cour des comptes*, p. 27, also points out that a large number of members of the prefectoral corps figure among special appointees to the Cour, but she sees nothing political in this fact. However, she does not look at the transitional service on a ministerial staff.

24. This decree superseded the decree of February 1, 1959, known as the Chatenet decree.

25. Philippe de Quinsac, "Des préfets. Mais quels préfets? " *Revue politique et parlementaire* (March 1971).

26. For a contrary view, see Vincent Wright, "Politics and Admini-

stration under the French Fifth Republic," *Political Studies* (March 1974):55 ff.

Chapter 6

1. See Pierre Corbel, *Le Parlement et le Plan* (Paris: Cujas, 1969).
2. Henry Ehrmann, "Les groupes d'intérêt et la bureaucratie dans les démocraties occidentales," *Revue française de sociologie* (September 1971):548.
3. See Jean Meynaud, *Nouvelles Etudes sur les groupes de pression en France* (Paris: Armand Colin, 1962), pp. 266-79. More recently, see Ezra Suleiman, *Power, Politics, and Bureaucracy*, chap. 7.
4. John Armstrong emphasizes the unique training received by top bureaucrats in France as compared with that of bureaucrats in other European countries. See his *The European Administrative Elite* (Princeton: Princeton University Press, 1973), pp. 194 ff.
5. Jean-Francois Kessler, "Les anciens élèves de l'ENA," *Revue française de science politique* (November 1964):248-49.
6. To use a self-styled "nonideological" expression employed by Karl Deutsch in his systematic analysis of politics. See his "Le gouvernement en tant que système de pilotate," in Pierre Birnbaum and François Chazel, eds., *Sociologie politique* (Paris: Armand Colin, 1971), vol. 1.
7. Guy Palmade, *Capitalisme et Capitalistes français au XIXe siècle* (Paris: Armand Colin, 1961).
8. Maurice Levy-Leboyer, "Le patronat francais a-t-il été malthusien?" *Le Mouvement social* (July-September 1974):18.
9. Charles de Gaulle, *Mémoires d'espoir*, vol. 1, *Le Renouveau, 1958-1962* (Paris: Plon, 1970), p. 143.
10. Michel Debré, "Press Conference," December 4, 1961, *Le Monde*, December 6, 1961.
11. See Yves Ullmo, "France," in John Hayward and Michael Watson, eds., *Planning, Politics, and Public Policy* (Cambridge, England: Cambridge University Press, 1975), p. 49.
12. See Henri Sevin, "Pouvoir politique et Industrialisation sous la Ve République" (thesis, presented to our graduate seminar at the University of Paris I in 1975).
13. General Assembly of the CNPF, January 19, 1965, in *Patronat*, February 1965, p. 7.
14. Concerning the techniques for insuring economic competition (FIFI model, etc.), see David Liggins, *National Economic Planning in France* (Farnborough: Saxon House, 1975), chaps. 4 and 5. The author also shows how during the Sixth Plan businessmen wished to place limits on the growth of the state sector (p. 147).
15. Lucien Nizard, *Planification et Société* (Presses Universitaires de Grenoble, 1974), p. 24.

16. Gilles Martinet, *Le Système Pompidou* (Paris: Editions du Seuil, 1973), p. 44.
17. *Le Monde*, March 1, 1969.
18. Lionel Stoleru, *L'Impératif industriel* (Paris: Editions du Seuil, 1969), p. 166. As an example of the neoliberal tendency, see Claude Alphandery, *Pour nationaliser l'Etat* (Paris: Editions du Seuil, 1968), p. 202. See also Jack E. S. Hayward, "State Intervention in France: the Changing Style of Government in Industrial Relations," *Political Studies* 3(1972):294 ff.
19. *1985. La France face au choc du futur* (publication of the Commissariat général du Plan, 1972), p. 164.
20. *Le Monde*, July 2, 1976.
21. Ibid.
22. Ehrmann, *Business Organizations;* see also Lavau, "Note sur un 'pressure group' français."
23. Stanley Hoffmann, *Le Mouvement Poujade* (Paris: Armand Colin, 1956), p. 400.
24. Christian Baudelot, Roger Establet, and Jacques Malemort, *La Petite Bourgeoisie en France* (Paris: Maspero, 1974), p. 121.
25. Libre-Service actualités, *Atlas des super et hyper* (December 1974), a study carried out under the auspices of AFRESCO.
26. Similarly, Pierre Abelin, president of the Société française des supermarchés, did not vote against according considerable power to the *départemental* commissions.
27. *Le Monde*, October 7-8, 1973.
28. See Libre-Service actualités, *Atlas*, pp. 66-72.
29. For what follows we have relied in part on the thesis of Charles Barucq, "L'Espace positionnel des membres des commissions d'industrialisation sous la Ve République" (presented to our graduate seminar at the University of Paris I in 1975).
30. Concerning the notion of "positional space," see Pierre Bourdieu, Luc Boltanski, and Monique de Saint-Martin, "Les stratégies de reconversion," *Informations sur les sciences sociales* 12(October 1973); and Luc Boltanski, "L'espace positionnel: multiplicité des positions institutionelles et habitus de classe," *Revue française de sociologie* (January-March 1973).
31. Under the Sixth Plan this proportion was 60 percent, considerably higher than under earlier commissions.
32. See the preceding chapter for our study of special appointments to the Grands Corps.
33. Bourdieu et al., "Les stratégies," p. 66.
34. See Gérard Grunberg, "L'Ecole polytechnique et ses Grands Corps," *Annuaire international de la fonction publique* (1973-74), pp. 401 ff.

35. Bourdieu et al., "Les stratégies," p. 74. It is unfortunate that the authors do not indicate exactly what proportion of their sample was of public firms (cf. table 17), so that their personnel might be distinguished from that of private firms.

36. See Erhard Friedberg, "Administration et entreprises," *Où va l'administration française* (Paris: Editions d'organisation, 1974), pp. 135 ff. See also Dominique Montjardet, "Carrière des dirigeants et contrôle de l'entreprise," *Sociologie du travail* 2(1975):52. Concerning the Ecole Polytechnique and the ENA, see Jacques Kosciusko-Morizet, *La "Mafia" polytechnicienne* (Paris: Editions du Seuil, 1973), pp. 114-19.

37. It should be noted that 27 percent of those leaving the prefectoral corps went into another department of the bureaucracy. Ten became trésoriers-payeurs généraux, fourteen joined the Conseil d'Etat, fourteen went to the Cour des comptes, and five entered the diplomatic corps.

38. See François Morin, *La Structure financière du capitalisme français* (Paris: Calmann-Levy, 1974), p. 95.

39. Recall, moreover, that members of presidential and prime ministerial staffs go mainly into banking and the mass media. See Badie and Birnbaum, "L'autonomie des institutions politico-administratives," p. 289.

40. Our sample consisted of the newspapers *Le Monde, Le Figaro, L'Aurore, France-Soir,* and *Le Parisien libéré;* the publishing house Hachette; the newsmagazine *L'Express;* the TV networks TF1, Antenne 2, and FR 3; and the radio networks Radio France and Europe 1.

41. Table 6.3 also shows the large number of diplomatic personnel going into the cultural sector; one reason for this is that many diplomats are educated at the Ecole normale supérieure and come to the diplomatic corps either via the normal channels or via integration. Another point to notice is that a great many members of the prefectoral corps go into the regional development and transportation sectors, that is, into private or public firms situated in the provinces and from which it is often possible to exert local political influence.

42. Daniel Derivery, "The Managers of Public Enterprises in France," in Dogan, ed., *The Mandarins of Western Europe,* pp. 222-23.

43. Here we are relying on a thesis by Philippe Ingal-Montagnier, "Les Dirigeants d'entreprises publiques en France" (presented to our graduate seminar at the University of Paris I, 1974).

44. Considering only company presidents, forty-one in all, fifteen of them in the public sector and twenty-six in the private, ten of the latter coming from the public sector, we find that no public-sector president came from the private sector, a fact which tends to reinforce the distinctive functional character of the state. Both public-sector presi-

dents and those in the private sector who worked first in the public sector hold multiple positions quite frequently; by contrast, presidents exclusively formed in the private sector are usually confined to that sector. Once again, then, it is much more common to proceed from the bureaucracy to capture positions in other areas than it is to do the opposite. Finally, private individuals moving from private firms to positions of responsibility in public firms in our sample came, it should be noted, from very large private firms, such as Pennaroya, La Paternelle, Paribas, Rothschild, Total, Palmolive, and so forth. Similarly, private firms that hired senior bureaucrats also holding posts in public firms included Pont-à-Mousson, Saint-Gobain, Suez, Rhône-Poulenc, and the Banque de l'Union parisienne. Thus the private-sector firms appearing in our sample are among the largest.

Chapter 7

1. Rémond, *La Droite en France,* pp. 281 ff.
2. See Jean-Claude Colliard, *Les Républicains indépendants* (Paris: Presses Universitaires de France, 1971), p. 247.
3. See Jean Charlot, *Le Phénomène gaulliste* (Paris: Fayard, 1970), pp. 68-75.
4. Cayrol et al., *Le Député français,* p. 51.
5. Jean Becarud, "Noblesse et représentation parlementaire 1871-1968," *Revue française de science politique* (October 1973):991.
6. Cayrol et al., *Le Député français,* pp. 81, 108, and 119-20.
7. Mark Kesselman has analyzed the socioprofessional background of members and leaders of the UDR and has shown that a very large segment of the party is drawn from the "lower middle classes," with workers representing a nonnegligible component. See his "Systèmes de pouvoir et cultures politiques au sein des partis politiques français. Le cas du PS et de l'UDR," *Revue française de sociologie* (October-December 1972):491-92.
8. Colette Ysmal, Daniel Boy, Gérard Grunberg, Béatrice Moine-Roy, "La redistribution des électeurs de droite en mai 1974," *Revue française de science politique* (April 1975):256.
9. The only minister who was not a senior bureaucrat and yet managed to remain a minister under Giscard's presidency was Christian Bonnet, who is not a traditional notable but an industrialist, the son of an industrialist, a doctor in law, and has had no lengthy career in local politics. Hence he shared the attributes characteristic of the new RI ministers.
10. Among the latter are Alice Saunier-Seïté, René Haby, Simone Veil, and General Bigeard.
11. See Antoni and Antoni, *Les Ministres de la Ve République,* p. 73.

12. It should also be noted that the ministers in the Chirac government were often personally connected in one way or another with Valéry Giscard d'Estaing. Some of them had served on his staff at the finance ministry: J.-P. Fourcade, L. Stoleru, M. Poniatowski. Others had held leadership positions in the RI, which Giscard revamped in 1968 and 1969: J.-P. Soisson, M. d'Ornano.

13. See Badie and Birnbaum, "L'autonomie des institutions politico-administratives," pp. 289 and 292. The figures given are for the composition of the cabinet in 1974.

14. An Enarch who had worked in the private sector, Jean François-Poncet, was brought in to replace Claude-Pierre Brossolette. The latter remained, as often happened, within the state sector, being named to head the Crédit lyonnais. If we are to believe *Le Point* (February 23, 1976, p. 47), however, big businessmen are almost never received at the Elysée.

15. See Jean-Marie Cotteret et al., *Giscard d'Estaing–Mitterrand, 54,774 mots pour convaincre* (Paris: Presses universitaires de France, 1976), pp. 96–97.

16. Michel Poniatowski, *Conduire le changement* (Paris: Fayard, 1975), p. 98.

17. Concerning the "end-of-ideology" school, see Pierre Birnbaum, *La Fin du politique* (Paris: Editions du Seuil, 1975). The language used by the leaders of the present majority contains themes identical to those current in the United States in the fifties, when that country was enjoying rapid economic growth.

18. For a critical analysis of this language and its claim to neutrality, see Pierre Bourdieu and Luc Boltanski, "La production de l'idéologie dominante," *Actes de la recherche en sciences sociales* (June 1976).

19. On the present [1976—trans.] steering committee of the clubs, there are five ENA graduates and five former members of Giscard's staff at the finance ministry, some of whom are also ENA graduates.

20. See Jean-Claude Thoenig, *L'Ere des technocrates* (Paris: Editions d'organisation, 1973), p. 272.

21. By contrast, not a single senior bureaucrat who graduated from the ENA or Polytechnique is found among the outgoing cabinet members belonging to the RI or presidential majority.

22. It is true that Olivier Guichard was briefly named prefect by special appointment. He cannot, however, be regarded a senior civil servant in the strict sense.

23. The third UDR member to enter the government, Antoine Rufenacht, did attend the ENA, but more importantly he had a long experience in party politics and had spent little time in bureaucratic posts. What is more, he was made responsible for preparations for the 1978 legislative elections.

24. It is significant that the new secretary of state assigned to the minister of industry and research in December 1976, Claude Coulais, a member of the RI, was himself a corporate officer. The man he was named to assist, Michel d'Ornano, was also a businessman with interests in the private sector.

25. *Le Monde,* September 8, 1976.

26. Ibid., September 23, 1976.

27. On the other hand, it is known that Jacques Chaban-Delmas was in favor of the capital gains law, as was Jean-Jacques Servan-Schreiber, who, following the government reshuffle and the departure of Jacques Chirac, reaffirmed his support for Giscardism (see *L'Express,* August 30–September 5, 1975, pp. 40–42). The rapprochement between the Giscardian majority and Jacques Chaban-Delmas may have been behind the inclusion of some of Chaban-Delmas's former collaborators on certain ministerial staffs. On Raymond Barre's staff, for example, besides Daniel Doustin—chief of staff, who had not been a direct associate of Chaban but had nevertheless been prefect of Aquitaine just prior to his nomination—we find several individuals who served on ministerial staffs in the Chaban government. Similarly, in both the government and on the staffs there was a large number of associates of Olivier Guichard, himself closely tied to Chaban: among the new ministers, Ruffenacht and Ligot had served on Guichard's staffs in the Ministry of National Education and the Ministry of Industry. Similarly, chief of staff Christian Beullac had served on Guichard's staff. We are dealing with a small number of men, who maintained their alliances over a long period of time.

28. In the prefectural assignments of September 1976, for example, Xavier Gouyou-Beauchamps was named, at thirty-nine years of age, prefect of the Ardèche, after serving on Giscard's staffs at the finance ministry and the Elysée from 1969 on, even though he had never been a subprefect. Similarly, Jean-Pierre Dupont, also only thirty-nine years of age, was named prefect of Corrèze after having served as secretary-general of this department in 1970 and later as chief of staff under Jacques Chirac, then prime minister, but now once more deputy from Corrèze. The relatively high number of prefects named as staff heads in the Barre government is also worthy of note: this was the case with the staffs of Barre, Beullac, and Stirn, among others. Finally, prominence should be given to Giscardism's growing influence over the prefectoral corps, which began with the May 1974 elections. On June 12 assignments were made involving twenty-one posts (twenty-six new assignments), especially concentrated in *départements* in which the left had made gains. These were punishments being handed out, nothing less. The fate of prefect Chadeau, who had the misfortune to support Chaban in this period, is typical and rather paradoxical to contemplate today, now

that alliances have been reversed. A further sign of the politicization of the prefectoral corps is the nomination of Michel Grollemund, former prefect of Gard and of the Languedoc-Roussillon region, to head the majority list in Nîmes in the March 1977 municipal elections.

Postscript

1. *Le Monde,* September 26, 1981.
2. In 1978 Nicos Poulantzas asked, "how could the Socialist Party avoid becoming a ruling mass party? Of course a Socialist-ruled state would surely not be the same as a state ruled by the Giscardians. But even apart from the nature of the party in power, the institutional situation of a ruling party involves limitations on democratic control and various liberties" (*L'état, le pouvoir, le socialisme* [Paris: Presses Universitaires de France, 1978], pp. 265–66).
3. See *Le Monde,* June 23–27, and August 8, 1981. On the ministerial staffs, see *Le Point,* September 7, 1981. Concerning changes in political personnel from 1958 to 1980, see Véronique Aubert and Jean-Luc Parodi, "Le personnel politique français," *Projet* (July-August 1981); and François de Baecque, "L'interpénétration des pouvoirs administratifs et politiques," in F. de Baecque and J.-L. Quermonne, eds., *Administration et politique sous la Cinquième République* (Paris: Presses de la Fondation Nationale des Sciences Politiques, 1981).
4. Pierre Birnbaum, *Le peuple et les gros. Histoire d'un mythe* (Paris, 1979).
5. J. Fabre, F. Hincker, L. Sève, *Les communistes et l'Etat* (Paris: Editions Sociales, 1977), p. 13.
6. See for example Michel Charzat and Ghislaine Toutain, *Le CERES, Un combat pour le socialisme* (Paris: Calmann-Levy, 1977).
7. Jules Guesde, *Etat, politique et morale de classe* (Paris: Giard et Brière, 1901 [1884]), pp. 52 and 92.
8. Jean Jaurès, *L'armée nouvelle,* vol. 4 of *Oeuvres completes,* p. 357.
9. *Le Monde,* May 7, 1981.
10. *Le Monde,* October 22, 1981.
11. *Le Monde,* September 22, 1981.
12. The Commissaire de la République does, however, have the right to appeal actions of the local authorities which he considers in excess of their mandate to the competent administrative tribunals. Furthermore, the distribution of powers among the various local authorities remains far from clear.

Index

Abelin, Pierre, 97
Alain, 55
Anthonioz, Marcel, 113, 118
Arago, 17
Armand-Rueff Committee, 93
Aron, Raymond, 91
Arrondissement system, 24
Autonomy. *See* Independence, state

Banking, 71, 108–9, 120, 147
Barre, Raymond, 119–20, 121, 132–33, 135, 144–45
Barrès, Maurice: *Les Déracinés*, 19
Baudelot, Christian, 93
Baumgartner, W., 66, 121
Benouville, Pierre de, 96
Bettencourt, André, 113–14, 118
Beullac, Christian, 132
Bigeard, M., 121
Bloch-Lainé, François, 89
Bodiguel, Jean-Luc, 68
Boisdé, M., 97
Boltanski, Luc, 103
Bonapartism, 4–8
Bonnet, Christian, 118
Boscary-Monservin, Robert, 113
Boulin, Robert, 133
Bourdieu, Pierre, 103
Bourgeoisie, grande, 4, 6–7, 8, 72, 116; in the Fifth Republic, 9, 11; in the Fourth Republic, 40; in the July Monarchy, 14, 16; in the Third Republic, 17, 20, 29–30
Boutmy, Emile, 29
Brossolette, Claude-Pierre, 110

Brousse, Pierre, 135
Bureaucracy, state, 1, 37–38, 50; and the business sector, 34–35, 39–40, 44, 56–57, 70–71, 90, 98–104, 129–30; career development of, 37, 39, 56–58, 102–3; and economic planning, 84–86, 88–90; in the Fifth Republic, 47–54, 65–68, 78, 86–92, 98–111; in the Fourth Republic, 31, 33, 40–44, 45; and Giscardism, 114–16, 118–20; and the Grands Corps, 72–83; independence of, 5–7, 12, 41, 85; membership of, 29–30, 40, 65–70; and the ministry, 33–34, 41–42, 65–71, 121–22; and "pantouflage," 103–6, 108–9; and politicians, 15–18, 29–31, 40–44, 63–71, 118–21, 131–32; and the public sector, 70–71, 109–11; and the Socialist government, 144–47; in the Third Republic, 18, 25–28, 29–30, 45
Bureaucrats, petty, 24, 28, 31, 37, 47
Business: and the Fifth Republic, 52–55, 58–64, 84–92, 98–111; and the Fourth Republic, 14, 28–29, 33–36, 38, 39, 42–44; and Giscardism, 114, 119, 123, 125–27, 129–30, 134; and modernization, 93–94, 97–98, 99; national versus international, 10–12, 86–87, 130–31; and "pantouflage," 103–6, 108–9; and regional development, 62–

63; small versus large, 86–88, 90, 92, 93–98, 99, 123; and the Socialist government, 146–47, 148. *See also* Capitalism; Economic planning

Capitalism, state monopoly, 9–12, 86–87, 134, 146. *See also* Business
Capitant, R., 112
Carnot, Sadi, 17
Casanova, Jean, 10, 134
Cavaillé, M., 118
Cayrol, Roland, 49
Censitaire system, 14, 17
Centre de démocrates sociaux (CDS), 135
Centre national des indépendants (CNI), 112–13
Chaban-Delmas, Jacques, 65, 70–71, 122, 135
Chamant, Jean, 113, 118
Chamber of Deputies, 14–15
Chapot, V., 115
Charbonnel, J., 121
Chatenet, P., 66, 121
Chenot, B., 66, 121
Chevènement, Jean-Pierre, 144
Chinaud, Roger, 97, 115
Chirac, Jacques, 92, 119, 121–23, 133, 134, 136
Civil servants. *See* Bureaucracy
Claude, Henri, 9
Clemenceau, 25
Colbertism, 86, 92
Combes, 25
Comité d'Information et de Défense—Union nationale des travailleurs indépendants (CIN UNATI), 94–95, 97
Commission on Growth, Employment, and Investment (1975), 101–2
Commissions d'Industrialisation du Plan, 98–102
Communist party, French (PCF), 9–12, 33, 45, 87, 133–34; membership of, 24, 31; and the Socialist government, 144–46
Confédération générale des petites et moyennes entreprises (PME), 11, 43–44, 86–88, 92; and Giscardism, 127, 128, 133, 134, 136
Conseil d'Etat, 15, 41–42, 67–68, 73–78; and the business sector, 76, 78, 106, 108; membership of, 16, 29, 72, 78. *See also* Grands Corps
Conseil national du patronat français (CNPF), 43, 76, 90, 92, 126
Conseils généraux, 16, 54, 147
Constitution of 1958, 45–46, 55, 58, 143
Corps of Engineers, 42. *See also* Grands Corps
Coty, Réné, 34, 46
Council of Ministers, 73–74
Council on Industrial Progress (1967), 91
Cour des comptes, 15, 41–42, 72–73; and the business sector, 103, 106–8; membership of, 16, 29–30, 78–80. *See also* Grands Corps
Cousin, Victor, 14
Couve de Murville, Maurice, 65, 66, 95, 97, 112; staff of, 70–71
Crozier, Michel, 91

Dahl, Robert, 19
Daladier, Edouard, 25
Darbel, Alain, 68
Daspercit, Gabriel, 96
Debré, Michel, 65, 70–71, 112; and economic planning, 85, 86, 88–89, 91, 92; and the Royer Law, 95, 97
de Broglie, Jean, 114, 118
de Gaulle, Charles, 9, 46; and the business sector, 85–86, 88, 91; ministry of, 66, 70, 121. *See also* Gaullism
Delouvrier, Paul, 91
Le Député français, 49, 51

Destremeau, B., 118, 119
Dijoud, Paul, 115, 118
Diplomatic corps, 42, 106, 107.
    See also Grands Corps
Doctors, 21-24, 28, 33, 47, 52, 145
Dogan, Matei, 66
Dorlhac, Helen, 118, 128
Ducray, G., 118
Dupont-Fauville, M., 110
Durafour, Michel, 97

Ecole libre des sciences politiques, 29, 72
Ecole national d'administration (ENA), 8, 9, 40; and the business sector, 85-86; 103, 110; and family ties, 69, 110; and the Fifth Republic, 60, 65, 68, 121; and Giscard's staff, 121-22, 125, 127, 132-33, 145; and the Grands Corps, 68-69, 72-73, 78, 82; and the Independent Republicans, 114, 115, 116, 118, 119, 120; and the Socialist government, 144-45, 147
Ecole Navale, 25
Ecole Polytechnique, 25, 65, 103, 132
Economic Development Committee (1965), 90
Economic planning, 84-102; and the Ecole Nationale d'Administration, 85-86; and Giscardism, 125-27, 130-31; and the Third through Sixth Plans, 88-92, 99-102. See also Business
Ehrmann, Henry, 84
Empire, Second, 4-9, 16, 21
Enarchs. See Ecole nationale d'administration
Establet, Roger, 93

Farmers, 36, 37
Fifth Republic, 28, 39; and the bureaucracy, 47-54, 65-68, 78, 86-92, 99-111; and the business sector, 52-55, 58-64, 84-92, 98-109; and centralization, 45-46, 59, 60, 84-87; governing elite in, 45-64, 117-21.
    See also Gaullism; Giscardism
Fontanet memorandum (1951), 93
Fourastié, Jean, 125
Fourcade, Jean-Pierre, 118-19, 120, 121, 125; and the *Perspectives et Realité* clubs, 127-28
Fournière, Xavier de la, 115
Fourth Republic, 18, 28-29, 31-45, 67, 142
François-Poncet, Jean, 120, 121
Frey, Roger, 112
Functionaries. See Bureaucrats

Galbraith, John Kenneth, 88
Galichon, Pierre, 110
Gambetta, Léon, 18, 20, 25, 28, 29, 40
Garaud, Marie-France, 122-23
Gaullism, 8-12, 112, 129; and economic planning, 86-92, 95, 134; and Giscardism, 124-25, 129, 132. See also Fifth Republic
Germain, Henri, 28
Giscard d'Estaing, Valéry, 89, 91, 121-25; ministry of, 117-23, 128, 132-33; and the Royer Law, 94, 95, 97, 135
Giscardism, 112-37; and the bureaucracy, 114-16, 118-20, 123, 126; and the business sector, 114, 119, 123, 125-27, 129-30, 133-34; and coalitions in, 133-37; and economic planning, 125-27, 130-31; and the Independent Republicans, 112-21, 123, 128, 131-34; staff of, 118-23; and state independence, 128-32
Goulet, Daniel, 96
"Governing class," 6, 28
Grands Corps, 15, 18, 147; and the business sector, 72, 76, 78,

82, 103-11; and the Fifth Republic, 54, 65-67; and the Fourth Republic, 18, 40, 41-42, 67; membership of, 16, 29-30, 40, 68-70; and the ministry, 65-66, 67, 68; special appointments to, 72-83
Great Britain, 141-42
Grévy, Jules, 25
Gruson, Claude, 89
Guesde, Jules, 146
Guichard, Olivier, 133
Guillaumat, Pierre, 66, 91, 121
Guiringaud, Louis de, 132
Guizot, François, 14

Haby, Réné, 121
Halévy, Daniel, 17, 28
Hardy, Charles, 115
Hegel, G. W. F., 85
"Hegemonic class," 6, 28
Herriot, Edouard, 25
Hincker, Michel, 11
Hoffmann, Stanley, 93

Independence, state, 4-8, 11-12, 14-16, 138-142; and bureaucracy, 3, 5-7, 9, 12, 67-69, 83; and economic planning, 84-87, 90-92; and Gaullism, 8-13, 85-92, 129, 132, 142; and Giscardism, 129-30, 132-37, 142
Independent Republicans (RI), 96, 97; and Giscardism, 112-21, 123, 124, 127, 128, 131-34; membership of, 50-51, 112-17
Industrialists, 33, 47, 61, 103. See also Business
Inspection des Finances, 29, 40-42, 72; and the business sector, 103, 106-8; and the Cour des comptes, 79, 80; and Giscardism, 125, 126. See also Grands Corps

Jaurès, Jean, 146
Jeanneney, Jean-Marcel, 89
Jouvenel, Robert de, 18, 21, 30

Joxe, Louis, 66, 112, 121
Juillet, Pierre, 122-23, 134
July Monarchy, 14-16, 18, 20, 21, 41, 138, 142

Kriegel-Valrimont, 10

Labor Party (British), 141-42
Lafitte, Jacques, 14
Lamartine, Alphonse de, 17
Lawyers, 33, 47, 52, 114, 145; in the Third Republic, 21-24, 25, 28
Lecanuet, Jean, 97, 122
Lecat, J.-P., 121
Ledru-Rollin, 17
Le Pors, Anicet, 147
Levy-Leboyer, Maurice, 88
Lewandowski, Olgierd, 50
Lhomme, Jean, 17, 29
Ligot, Maurice, 132
Lipset, Seymour Martin, 19
Louis XIV, 86
Louis-Philippe, 14

MacMahon, Patrice de, 17
Malemort, Jacques, 93
Mallet, Serge, 11
Malraux, André, 112
Marcellin, R., 113, 118
Marchais, Georges, 133
Martin, R., 91
Martinet, Gilles, 90
Marx, Karl, 4-8
Massé, Pierre, 89
Mass media, 62, 71, 109
Mauroy, Pierre, 144-45
Messmer, Pierre, 65, 66, 70-71, 112
Michelet, E., 112
Military, 5, 30
Mills, C. Wright, 61
Ministry: of Barre, 132-33; and the bureaucracy, 41-42, 52, 65-71, 82-83; and the business sector, 38-39, 52-54, 58-64, 70-71, 103; career development of, 58-64; of Chirac, 119, 121-

23; in the Fifth Republic, 45–46, 52–55, 58–63, 117–21; in the Fourth Republic, 33–34, 38–39, 41–42; of Giscard, 117–23, 128, 132–33; of Mauroy, 144–45; membership of, 61, 65, 67, 70–71, 121; and parliament, 25–28, 33–34, 45–46, 52–55, 66–70, 120–22; in the Third Republic, 25–28
Mitterrand, François, 124, 143, 146
Mondon, Raymond, 113, 114, 115, 118
Mosca, Gaetano, 17, 20
Mouvement républicain populaire (MRP), 35, 39

Napoleon III, 4–8, 86
Nicoud, Gerard, 94
Nizard, Lucien, 90
Nora, Simon, 90

Organisation de l'Armée secrète (OAS), 113
Orleanists, 113
Ornano, Michel d', 115, 118, 119, 130
Ortoli-Montjoie commission, 100

Palmade, Guy, 87
"Pantouflage," 71, 103–9, 120. *See also* Business
Paquet, Aimé, 114, 118
Parodi, Jean-Luc, 49
Parti républicain radical et radical-socialiste. *See* Radical party
Paye, L., 66, 121
Pelletan, Camille, 25
Périer, Casimir, 14
Perronnet, Gabriel, 97
Perspectives et Realité Clubs, 124–28, 129, 131
Peyrefitte, A., 121
Pinay, Antoine, 10–11, 86, 113, 134
Politicians, 1, 6, 16–30, 145; and the bureaucracy, 15–17, 31, 46–47, 52, 66; and the business sector, 28–29, 34–39, 43–44, 47, 56; career development of, 34–38, 55–58; and economic planning, 84, 89; in the Fifth Republic, 45–51, 54–64, 66, 131–32; in the Fourth Republic, 31–38; and Giscardism, 112–18, 120–21, 133–37; and the liberal professions, 21–25, 31, 38, 47–49; and local politics, 24–25, 35–36, 54–55, 56–57; and the middle classes, 17, 18, 20–21, 31, 47–49; and the ministry, 25–30, 33–34, 45–46, 52–55, 66–71, 118–21; social background of, 31–33, 47–51, 57; and the workers, 31, 47–48
Pompidou, Georges, 65, 70–71, 87, 121–23, 134; and economic planning, 89, 90, 91, 94
Poniatowski, Michel, 115, 118, 125, 128
Poperin, Jean, 96
Popular Front, 30
Postel-Vinay, André, 120
Poujadist movement, 93
Poulantzas, Nicos, 28
Powers, separation of, 1, 6, 15–16, 141–44; in the Fifth Republic, 45–46, 52–55, 64–69, 84–87; in the Fourth Republic, 31–34, 40–44; and Giscardism, 118–21, 131–32; in the Third Republic, 17, 25–30. *See also* Ministry; Politicians
Prefectural corps, 40–42, 75–76, 79–82, 106–7, 147. *See also* Grands Corps
President of the Republic, 45, 46, 143–44
Présidents du conseils, 42, 147
Prime ministers, 65–66. *See also* Ministry
Professionals, liberal: in the Fifth Republic, 47, 52; in the Fourth Republic, 31, 33, 38, 39; in the Third Republic, 21–24, 25, 28

Index

Pronteau, Jean, 10, 11
Public sector, 62-63, 70-71, 106-7, 109-11

Quilès, Paul, 146

Radical party, 18-20, 21-24, 28, 35, 135
Régie pour Favoriser la Productivité (RFP), 35, 39, 45, 46, 59-60, 136
Resistance, 31, 112, 117
Républicains Indépendants. *See* Independent Republicans
Rolland, Hector, 134
Roux, Ambroise, 91
Royer, Jean, 94, 95, 96, 136
Royer Law, 93-98, 101, 135

Saint-Cyr, 25
Saint-Martin, Monique de, 103
Saunier-Seité, A. 121
Sauvagnargues, J. 121
Schnapper, Dominique, 68
Schumpeter, Joseph A., 17, 19, 21
Segard, Norbert, 128
Servan-Schreiber, Jean-Jacques, 97
Servin, Marcel, 10, 11, 134
Siegfried, André, 25, 40
Siwek-Pouydesseau, Jeanne, 75
Socialist party (PS), 51, 143-48
Socialist party (SFIO), 24, 31, 35, 37, 39
Soisson, Jean-Pierre, 115, 118, 119
Spoils system, 17, 147
Statism, 4-12, 142-44, 147-48; and economic planning, 84-87, 89-92; in the Fifth Republic, 45-46, 55, 60
Stirn, O., 121
Stoleru, Lionel, 92, 119-20, 121; *L'Imperatif industriel*, 91

Taittinger, P.-C., 118, 119
Tardieu, André, 19, 21
Teachers: in the Fifth Republic, 47, 52; in the Fourth Republic, 31, 33, 37; in the Socialist government, 144-46; in the Third Republic, 21-24, 25, 28
Third Republic, 16-30, 32-33, 41, 142
Thibaudet, Albert, 19-20, 21
Thiers, Adolphe, 14-15
Thorez, Maurice, 10, 11-12
Tinaud, J.-L., 118
Tocqueville, Alexis de, 5
Tudesq, André-Jean, 16

Union pour la défense de la République (UDR), 39, 122, 123, 128; in the Fifth Republic, 50-51, 59-60; and Giscardism, 112, 115, 127, 132-35; membership of, 115, 116-17

Veil, Simone, 121, 128
Villemain, 14

Wahl, Nicholas, 46
Weber, Max, 6, 17, 20, 85
Wendel, François de, 28
Workers, 31, 33, 47-49, 74, 76, 145

Ysmal, Colette, 49